PHILIPPINES

...UNEI SABAH
...S...IA
...RAWAK

...ORNEO MOLUCCAS
N E S I A
SULAWESI

...DURA
FLORES
BALI
LOMBOK SUMBAWA
SUMBA TIMOR

IMAGES OF ASIA

Javanese Shadow Puppets

Titles in the series

Balinese Paintings (2nd edn.)
A. A. M. DJELANTIK

Bamboo and Rattan:
Traditional Uses and Beliefs
JACQUELINE M. PIPER

The Birds of Java and Bali
DEREK HOLMES and
STEPHEN NASH

The Birds of Sumatra and
Kalimantan
DEREK HOLMES and
STEPHEN NASH

Borobudur (2nd edn.)
JACQUES DUMARÇAY

Burmese Puppets
NOEL F. SINGER

Early Maps of South-East Asia
(2nd edn.)
R. T. FELL

Folk Pottery in South-East Asia
DAWN F. ROONEY

Fruits of South-East Asia: Facts
and Folklore
JACQUELINE M. PIPER

A Garden of Eden: Plant Life in
South-East Asia
WENDY VEEVERS-CARTER

Gardens and Parks of Singapore
VÉRONIQUE SANSON

The House in South-East Asia
JACQUES DUMARÇAY

Images of the Buddha in Thailand
DOROTHY H. FICKLE

Indonesian Batik: Processes,
Patterns and Places
SYLVIA FRASER-LU

Javanese Gamelan (2nd edn.)
JENNIFER LINDSAY

Javanese Shadow Puppets
WARD KEELER

The Kris: Mystic Weapon of the
Malay World (2nd edn.)
EDWARD FREY

Life in the Javanese Kraton
AART VAN BEEK

Mammals of South-East Asia
(2nd edn.)
EARL OF CRANBROOK

Musical Instruments of
South-East Asia
ERIC TAYLOR

Old Bangkok
MICHAEL SMITHIES

Old Manila
RAMÓN MA. ZARAGOZA

Old Penang
SARNIA HAYES HOYT

Old Singapore
MAYA JAYAPAL

Sarawak Crafts: Methods,
Materials, and Motifs
HEIDI MUNAN

Silverware of South-East Asia
SYLVIA FRASER-LU

Songbirds in Singapore:
The Growth of a Pastime
LESLEY LAYTON

Javanese Shadow Puppets

WARD KEELER

SINGAPORE
OXFORD UNIVERSITY PRESS
OXFORD NEW YORK
1992

Oxford University Press

*Oxford New York Toronto
Delhi Bombay Calcutta Madras Karachi
Kuala Lumpur Singapore Hong Kong Tokyo
Nairobi Dar es Salaam Cape Town
Melbourne Auckland
and associated companies in
Berlin Ibadan*

Oxford is a trade mark of Oxford University Press

© *Oxford University Press Pte. Ltd. 1992*

*Published in the United States by
Oxford University Press, Inc., New York*

All rights reserved. No part of this publication may be reproduced,
stored in a retrieval system, or transmitted, in any form or by any means,
electronic, mechanical, photocopying, recording or otherwise,
without the prior permission of Oxford University Press

ISBN 0 19 588585 6

British Library Cataloguing in Publication Data

A catalogue record for this book is available from the British Library

Library of Congress Cataloging-in-Publication Data
Keeler, Ward.
Javanese shadow puppets/Ward Keeler.
p.   cm.—(Images of Asia)
Includes bibliographical references.
ISBN 0-19-588585-6:
1. Wayang. 2. Shadow shows—Indonesia—Java. 3. Java
(Indonesia)—Social life and customs. I. Title. II. Series.
PN1979.S5K444   1992
791.5'3—dc20
                                                    92-9851
                                                    CIP

*Printed in Singapore by Kyodo Printing Co. (S) Pte. Ltd.
Published by Oxford University Press Pte. Ltd.,
Unit 221, Ubi Avenue 4, Singapore 1440*

Preface

WHEN I travelled to Java for the first time, in 1968, after my first year in college, I was pleased when a friend, Mas Siswanto Soedomo, invited me to go to a shadow puppet performance in Jogjakarta one Saturday night. Once at the performance, however, I recall feeling frustrated: when I asked my friend every few minutes what was happening, he answered, 'Nothing much'. A few years later, while living in a village on the outskirts of Jogjakarta, I was thrilled to discover that my efforts to learn the Javanese language had progressed far enough to enable me to understand a few phrases in a performance without tugging on anyone's sleeve for an explanation. But the more Javanese I learned and the more I understood of the performances I attended, the more I was aware that my impatience had been misplaced. A shadow play is a very verbal form of entertainment, and for the first forty minutes or so, just as my friend had assured me, virtually nothing happens. An avid opera fan, I saw in shadow plays a distant relative of that art form's grand mix of music, story, and extravagant stylization, but I was puzzled by the different sorts of conventions that shape a performance of shadow puppets, including its very deliberate pace. Returning to Java to do anthropological field work in 1988, I spent two years researching just that issue: what the aesthetic principles underlying the art form are, and how this very unusual and intriguing genre fits into its particular cultural setting. I lived with a puppeteer and his family for most of that time, learning about shadow plays and about Javanese culture, in conversation with them and their neighbours, and I attended performances put on by him and other puppeteers in Central Java. I look back on that time with great nostalgia, forgetting in retrospect the anxieties and difficulties

PREFACE

of doing research, and recalling many tropical nights filled with beautiful music, entertaining stories, and great snacks.

Writing a book, even a brief one, means running up debts to many people. Ki Anom Soeroto was kind enough to permit me to record the performance I describe in the first two chapters. Richard Lavine, Leslie Morris, Kathleen Stewart, and Samuel Wilson, gave me many suggestions on how to make this book more informative and readable. Maureen Aung-Thwin, H. Boediardjo, Jacques Dumarçay, Alan Feinstein, Judith Ferster, Sylvia Fraser-Lu, Edward Frey, Jennifer Lindsay, Leslie Morris, and Suharso, all took time and effort to provide illustrations. (Photographs without photo credits were taken by me.) To all of these people, I am very grateful.

Austin, Texas WARD KEELER
January 1992

Contents

Preface	*v*
Introduction	1
1 Pandhu Crowned King	5
2 *Wayang* in Javanese Society	38
3 The Repertoire of Stories and the Structure of the Performance	49
4 What Might *Wayang* Mean?	56
5 An Ancient Art Form in the Modern World	66
Select Bibliography	72

Introduction

AMONG Asia's many glories are its colourful and unusual performing arts. Yet none surpasses the Javanese shadow play in the strangeness of its format and, by virtue of that strangeness, the promise of aesthetic and perhaps even mystical riches to be found within it. That an art form should be based on shadows is already intriguing. Even aside from that, few art forms anywhere in the world stylize the human form as radically or impose as rigorous constraints on its practitioners as does the *wayang kulit* (shadow play) tradition. Its refined heroes with tiny waists and impossibly long arms, the big-nosed, pop-eyed giants (Plate 1), and the heroines with skirts that extend forward rather than trail behind them, these conventionalized images rule out any straightforward equivalences between the physical appearance of characters in the plays and the look of humans in life (Colour Plate 1). (It is indicative of how far the distortion of human features goes in shadow puppets that most Westerners are unable to distinguish male and female figures accurately until they acquire some familiarity with the tradition.) The stories that get told in performances concern gods, heroes, and monsters who are able to flout the usual limits on human capacities: many can fly, for example, and some control weapons of great magical potency (Plate 2). There is virtually no scenery, and the puppets themselves can be manipulated only very little. If Western arts, especially popular ones, have opted for a realistic style in which the successful imitation of 'real' life is ostensibly the standard to which performers are held, then shadow plays' radical departure from life as we know it clearly puts them across an enormous aesthetic divide.

It would be vain, and a bit deflating, to try to dispel the aura of strangeness that surrounds a Westerner's vision of Javanese shadow plays. Yet it is also true that shadow plays display

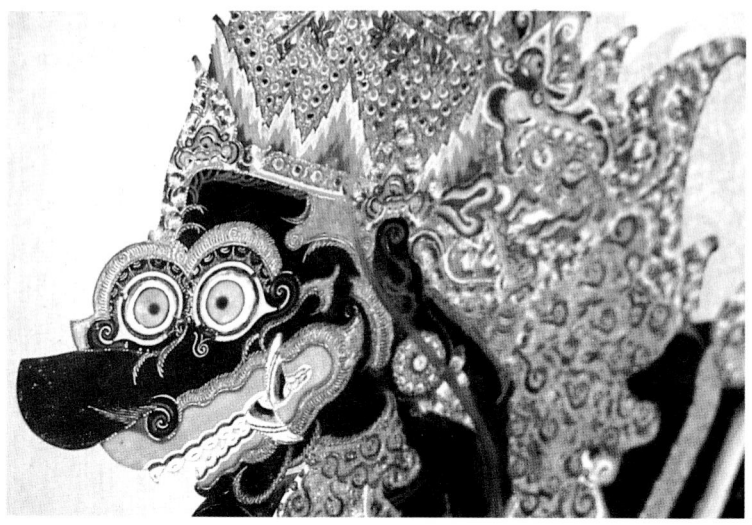

1. A demon king with coarse features and fangs.

aesthetic principles that are intelligible and even sensible to outsiders: they need not remain unapproachably exotic. To make them somewhat more accessible, it is worth considering the stories they relate, their place in Javanese social life, what Javanese have to say about them, what meanings both Javanese and foreign analysts have seen in them, and the place they may retain in Javanese society in future. The chapters that follow will address these topics in turn.

One brief caveat would not be out of place at the outset. To most Westerners, the word 'puppets' evokes pleasant images of performances seen in childhood, and of familiar figures—Punch and Judy, or Kermit the Frog—held dear to memory. In Java, children love puppets, too. But as they grow older, they need not lose track of the figures they came to know in countless performances in their childhood. On the contrary, Javanese get to know those characters better as they see them appear and reappear in every shadow play they attend throughout their lives. Some of the characters are as lovable and familiar as

INTRODUCTION

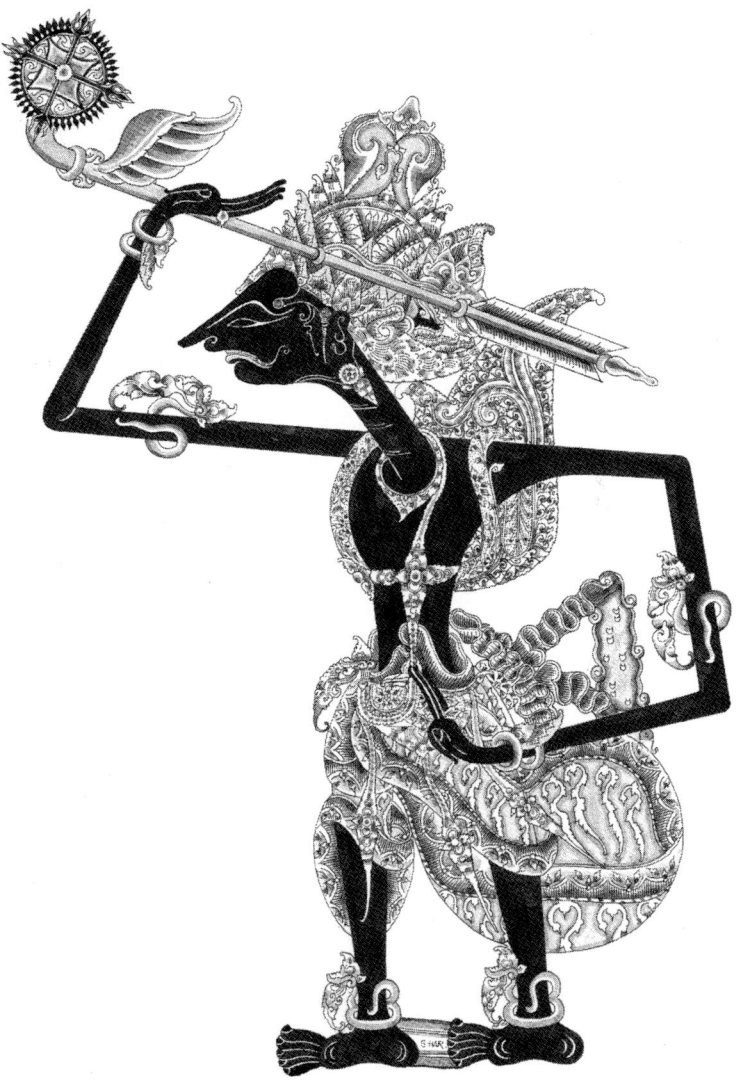

2. Kresna wields a terrifying weapon, the *cakra*, whose magical powers can be unleashed only by incarnations of the god Wisnu. (Drawing by Suharso)

Big Bird, while others are far more complex—perhaps heroic, perhaps cowardly, or even sinister. The stories in which they figure are by no means restricted to light and charming fantasies. They may, instead, turn on deadly serious histories of political rivalry, sexual jealousy, and bloodthirsty revenge. Javanese shadow plays are by no means entertainment intended primarily for children.

Wayang kulit is not the only performing art that flourishes in Java. At the royal courts, human dancers impersonate shadow puppets in a dance genre called *wayang wong* (human shadow puppets) (Colour Plate 2). Folk drama, in which human actors enact any of a great array of historical, fictional, even Shakespearian, Biblical, or other stories, are extremely popular, and attract the interest of more women than *wayang* does. Music concerts, such as of Javanese, Indonesian, and 'Muslim' pop music, often attract larger numbers of young people, especially among city-dwellers, than shadow plays.

Nevertheless, shadow plays enjoy the greatest prestige among all the arts in Java, so much so that *wayang* imagery crops up in many different media (Colour Plates 3 and 4). One reason for their prestige is that they are considered Java's oldest and therefore most venerable genre. The dean of Old Javanese studies, Father Zoetmulder, points to a reference to a performance of *wayang* in a royal charter issued in 907 of our era.[1] He warns that we cannot know for sure what the nature of that performance was. But a reference in a twelfth-century Javanese epic poem makes more explicit mention of spectators watching 'carved leather': clearly this shows that *wayang* were being given in Java 900 years ago.[2] In a society in which age necessarily garners respect, something so ancient is accorded enormous value. Yet, at the same time, shadow plays are found genuinely entertaining by a great many Javanese, young and old. Looking at a particular performance should help to see why.

[1] See Zoetmulder, 1974, pp. 208–9.
[2] Ibid., p. 210.

I
Pandhu Crowned King

WALKING along a road at night in Java, whether in town or in the countryside, one often hears a distinctive sound coming from an unseen loudspeaker. It is usually hard to figure out what direction it is coming from, but the sound consists of a man's voice, either singing or speaking, heard against the background of the Javanese percussion orchestra, or *gamelan*. At times the man sings long phrases while a soft, velvety sound provides subtle musical support. At other times the sound of the orchestra swells and a number of voices, both men's and women's, can be heard, in addition to the single male voice in the foreground. Then there are moments when the man's voice sounds like a drone, neither really speaking nor singing, intoning phrases with a rapid but uninflected delivery. Through it all, there is another, non-musical background, the sound of people speaking among themselves, some voices clearly those of children, plus a few dogs barking.

These are the sounds of a Javanese shadow play, or *wayang kulit*.[1] If it is still early, about nine or so at night, the various sorts of sounds just described continue for about twenty minutes, and someone walking along who heard them might feel interested in tracing them to their source. It is likely to be the dry season, sometime between April and November, and there may be a bright moon to light the way. The day was hot

---

[1] 'Javanese *wayang kulit*', usually referred to by Javanese (and in the text below) simply as *wayang*, refers to shadow plays as performed in Central and East Java. The word *wayang* in Javanese can refer to performances, to individual puppets, or to the tradition more generally, and no distinction is made in Javanese between singular and plural. *Wayang kulit* also exists in Bali and Lombok, while a rod puppet tradition, called *wayang golèk*, is popular among the Sundanese of West Java, as well as among some Javanese in the area west of Jogjakarta. Within the Javanese *wayang kulit* tradition, there are regional variations, most notably those of Jogjakarta, Surakarta, and Banyumas.

and dry but the air is cooling off quickly. Especially in the countryside, where entertainments are fewer than in town, going to see a *wayang* would be an enjoyable diversion.

Following a path through the fields, one would notice the sound changing. There is less singing to be heard. In its place there is a good deal of talking, in a number of different voices. The pace is very deliberate, but some voices are low-pitched and flat, without emphasis of any kind. One voice is shrill, another slurred and slow, yet another ponderous and deep. The background noise of people talking and moving about is clearer now, no longer covered by the sound of the *gamelan* orchestra, which has fallen silent. It seems clear that these people in the background, chatting away, are paying little attention to the performance. The voices in the foreground are clear, however, and one can start to listen to what is being said even while making one's way toward the bright lights visible in a hamlet in the distance.

'What might be the cause of your having come in such haste, King Kunthiboja?' The question is put in a deep voice, slowly and with great dignity.

'I wished first of all to visit my relatives here in the kingdom of Ngastina whom I have not seen for some time, and to offer you, King Abyasa, the humblest expression of my deeply felt respect. Further, I have come in response to the letter you were gracious enough to address to me, a letter in which you signalled the desire that I come accompanied by all the knights of my domain of Madura. Great was my concern, on reading this letter. For what reason would His Highness issue such a command, I wondered, and unable to find an answer, I came in all possible speed to pay you obeisance and await your orders.'

The conversation is interrupted by a series of sung phrases. A hush falls over the people who had been talking in the background, who appear to wait as anxiously as King Kunthiboja himself for King Abyasa's response.

'I am now an old man, and I have lost all taste for the onerous responsibilities of a king. I wish to deliver myself of that burden and, following the path of my father, Palasara, retreat to the mountain hermitage of Seven Peaks.'

'That is indeed the wont and the duty of kings. Yet I would ask whom you might name to succeed you as king of Ngastina?'

'It is my second son, Pandhu, to whom I will grant the kingship.'

'Might I inquire why you do not choose to entrust your authority instead to your elder son, Drestarata, since it is the eldest of a king's sons who is entitled to inherit the crown?'

'A king must be without flaw of any kind, spiritual or physical. My elder son, Drestarata, is blind. He cannot succeed me.'

'Ah indeed, I was in error. Might I also inquire when you wish to enter upon meditation in the hermitage?'

'Know, Kunthiboja, that I am resolved to do so at once. Yet there is an obstacle: my son Pandhu has left Ngastina without taking his leave. He has already been gone over a month and he has given no sign of his whereabouts. That is not the only source of my concern. Pandhu is the recipient of a challenge from the king of Ngalengkapura, King Wisamuka, who intends to kill Pandhu. Wisamuka claims that Pandhu killed his father, and either Pandhu must present himself for a duel, or Wisamuka will gather his troops and invade our kingdom of Ngastina.'

Reaching the scene of the performance at this moment, one would find a crowd sitting or standing before a house whose front wall has been removed (Plate 3). Inside the house, there is a long white screen with a red border and banana tree-trunks running along its base. Hundreds of flat, brightly painted figures have been placed against the screen in order of increasing size, starting near the centre of the screen—where they are only five or six inches in height—and going out to either side, beyond the edges of the screen—where some are over two feet tall. At the centre of the screen six or seven of these figures stand facing each other. Each one is secured in the banana

3. Early in a performance, a great many neighbours and passers-by watch from outside the house. Women in the audience are not likely to stay late, but a popular *dalang* will keep a large crowd of males watching for several hours.

tree-trunks below the screen by means of a long stem (Colour Plate 5). A man in Javanese dress—a batik cap, a dark jacket, and a batik skirt, with a Javanese dagger, or *kris*, tucked into the sash in the small of his back—sits cross-legged in front of the screen. This is the puppeteer, or *dalang*[2] (Plate 4). An electric light shines above his head, and to his left there is a large wooden box, its top removed. Behind him is arrayed the *gamelan* orchestra (Plate 5), in this case an unusually large and handsome set of instruments, and among them are the players, men sitting on mats, all dressed in formal Javanese attire (Colour Plate 6 and Plate 6).

The *dalang* reaches up to take the central stem of one of the characters out of the banana tree-trunk, while grasping two other, lighter sticks that are attached to the figure's hands (Colour Plates 7 and 8). The figure's arms, jointed at the shoulders and elbows, are exaggeratedly long, its waist narrow. Its eyes are round and a black moustache curls above and beyond the corners of its mouth. An elaborate crown rests upon its head, and ornaments embellish its chest, upper arms, and ankles. Moving the central stem with one hand, while working the two other stems with the other, the *dalang* endows the figure with slight, but nervous, movements.

'Do you believe, venerable king, that I, Kunthiboja, king of Madura, will permit this outrageous affront to the honour of your second son to be left unavenged? Any act, any remark, any look that does you or your lineage dishonour dishonours me. I cannot tolerate, I will not tolerate, such behaviour. Permit me to take my leave at once and challenge this presumptuous opponent to battle.'

Kunthiboja's speech has become agitated, his voice has risen in pitch and volume, matching the flailing gestures he makes

---

[2]The word is written *dhalang* in contemporary Javanese, because the initial consonant is made by raising the tip of the tongue to the roof of the mouth. But it is written *dalang* in Indonesian, and this has become the convention in English as well. Incidentally, many foreigners incorrectly stress the final syllable in such words as *dalang* and *wayang*, but Javanese has even syllable stress.

JAVANESE SHADOW PUPPETS

4. The puppeteer, or *dalang*, is dressed in formal Javanese attire, including the Javanese dagger, or *kris*, at his back. He is seated in front of the screen. (Drawing by Suharso)

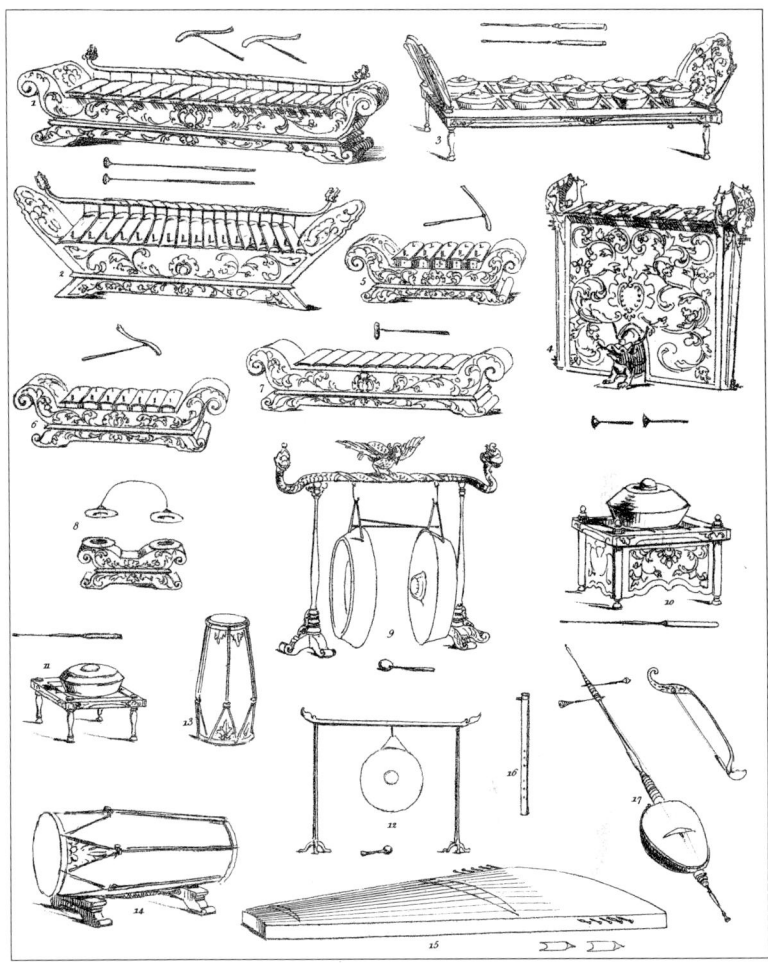

5. *Gamelan* instruments. (From Thomas Stamford Raffles, *The History of Java*, 1817)

6. Seated behind the puppeteer are the members of the orchestra, who must respond to a variety of cues from the *dalang* to know when to start and stop their playing. (Drawing by Suharso)

7. The *dalang* raps on the wooden puppet box to his left to punctuate dialogue and to signal the orchestra when to play. (Drawing by Suharso)

with his arms. Replacing the puppet in the banana tree-trunk, the *dalang* picks up a round-headed mallet with his left hand and raps it against the box to his left (Plate 7). With his right hand, he grasps the arm supports of the figure facing Kunthiboja. This figure resembles King Kunthiboja in that he too has a crown and elaborate ornaments. But his face is black, his eyes are narrow slits, and he wears shoes. He is made to gesture slightly with his hands as he speaks.

'Your words cause my heart to feel cool, relieved of its worry. Yet let me first offer you a feast to assuage the hunger you must feel after your journey from Madura.'

'Many thanks, but I cannot rest until I have driven off this pall that hangs over Ngastina. Please grant me leave to depart at once.'

The *dalang* raps the mallet against the puppet box and the *gamelan* begins to play, while King Kunthiboja bows deeply to King Abyasa and leaves. The *dalang* holds the puppet well away from the screen before putting it down next to him. He does this because he wishes to make it appear to people sitting behind the screen that the puppets move on their own—that there is no *dalang*. These people, whom one can glimpse sitting on straight-backed metal chairs beyond the rows of puppets to the sides of the screen, see only the shadows that the light above the *dalang*'s head makes the puppets cast, highly detailed black and white images on the screen's white surface. The fine gradations of colour and inked highlights visible on the puppets themselves are lost to observers of the shadows. But these spectators can see the elaborate designs created by perforating pieces of water buffalo hide in the making of a puppet (Plate 8), and they can enjoy the play on the size and clarity of the images that the *dalang* achieves by holding the puppets slightly further from or closer to the screen (Colour Plate 9 and Plate 9).

Inside the house, behind the screen, there are a few dozen men sitting observing the shadows. Outside there are hundreds more, and for them getting a good view of the performance is not so easy. To remedy matters, people in the rear of the

PANDHU CROWNED KING

8. In a time-honoured process, puppets are made by carving out pieces of water buffalo hide and then using picks to perforate them, creating intricate designs. (Judith Ferster)

9. On the shadow side of the screen, the colours are lost, but the intricacy of each figure's design is clearer. (Judith Ferster)

crowd start to cry out to those in front, *Lungguh! Lungguh!* (Sit! Sit!), urging them to squat on the ground so that everyone may see. Some people in front comply, others do not. The yelling grows louder. There is a problem, because the *gamelan* and screen are placed on a platform that rises a few feet off the ground. People standing right up near the platform will no longer be able to see if they sit down. They would be willing to do so only if they could move back a little. That is not easy when the crowd behind them is so large and people are packed together so densely. Children, meanwhile, want to stand right at the edge of the platform, or sit on the wooden runners that form something like a little fence around its edge. Eventually, things are sorted out: most of the crowd is sitting, children are chased off the platform, and most people have a fairly good view of the performance, even if at a considerable distance. This arrangement, however, is subject to change. People too far to either side of the seated assembly cannot see and they remain standing, leaning slightly to try to see inside the house where the screen is. As their numbers grow, they will begin to obstruct the view of people seated further back, who may be obliged to stand up if they wish to see anything more than the backs of those standing. Children, too, will soon begin to crowd up toward the platform again. There are likely to be moments of wrangling among elements of the crowd at several points in the performance. But for the moment there is a semblance of order.

King Abyasa remains on the screen after Kunthiboja's departure. He now speaks to another figure, this one with a black face, a large nose and round eyes, whom he addresses as Gandamana. Abyasa explains that the kingdom of Ngastina stands in need of a prime minister and Gandamana is well qualified for the post. No one, however, should attain high office without having first demonstrated his loyalty to the king through some impressive deed. Abyasa tells Gandamana to seek out Pandhu as the means to prove his dedication to the well-being of the realm: he should not return until he can do so escorting Pandhu. Abyasa then announces that he is bringing this royal audience to a close and will return to his private quarters.

The *dalang* takes each of the puppets out of the banana tree-trunk and removes it. King Abyasa leaves first, followed by two ladies-in-waiting, then other members of the court (Colour Plate 10). The *dalang* moves each puppet in a different manner, indicating each character's resoluteness, or impetuosity, or grace. He then mentions, though he does not yet show, Abyasa's two queens, Ambika and Ambiki, who await him in the royal chambers. When he stops speaking, a stringed instrument with a Middle Eastern quality to its tone plays a few phrases, and then the entire *gamelan* joins in. Behind and to the right of the *dalang* are three women and two men who now sing, the women taking separate turns, the men singing in unison (Colour Plate 11).

The *dalang* turns to pick up a glass filled with sweet tea. He sips for a moment, and then takes a cigarette out of a pack lying on the mat beside him and lights it. He is still young, only in his thirties, and his full cheeks as well as the ringing tones of his singing voice bring to mind a Western tenor. Actually, most people would recognize him more easily from the sound of his voice than from his face: his name is Ki Anom Soeroto, and he is currently the most popular *dalang* performing in the style of the court city of Solo (also known as Surakarta) in Central Java. His fame comes from his great comic inventiveness as well as his superb singing voice, and the hundreds of people who have come to watch his performance attest to the popularity he has achieved even at a relatively early age (Plate 10).

Ki Anom has only a few moments to relax because he will soon have to describe, in the low drone in which a *dalang* provides the background description of a scene, another set of characters. Resting, in fact, is the one thing a *dalang* does very little of in the course of a shadow play. He must manipulate all the puppets, and at the same time give them all their voices, imparting to each figure a distinct timbre and manner of speaking, as well as improvising all their remarks. He must fit

10. Ki Anom Soeroto, relaxing at home, tries out a new puppet he has just commissioned. Despite his youth, he is generally accorded top honours among contemporary Solonese *dalang*.

a particular story, sometimes a very complicated one, to the constraints of a rigid dramatic structure. This structure consists of a series of required scenes and set pieces, such as the opening at a royal court we have just seen. He must also direct the *gamelan* orchestra by means of subtle verbal cues and strokes of the mallet against the puppet box. At many points, while manipulating the puppets, he holds the mallet between the big and second toes of his right foot in order to strike a set of metal plates suspended from the side of the box: this creates a metallic, crashing noise with which he punctuates the action. Remarkably, the *dalang* must fulfil all of these responsibilities—scriptwriter, conductor, narrator, singer, manipulator of the puppets, and impersonator of all their voices—*all night*, since a Javanese shadow play begins at nine in the evening and lasts till dawn—about five or so the next morning—without intermission. He does so without so much as uncrossing his legs, since his right foot must be ready to strike the mallet against the puppet box. While the musicians and the people watching the performance from behind the screen all eat at least one meal, in some cases two, before morning, he eats nothing, taking only sweet tea and clove-scented cigarettes for refreshment. And as Javanese often remark with particular astonishment, he does not use the bathroom all night.

As Ki Anom introduces the scene in the king's chambers, he explains that the two queens are sisters, and that the elder, Ambika, has given birth to Drestarata, and the younger, Ambiki, to Pandhu. When the king and his two queens begin to speak, they review the conversations that occurred in the preceding scene, and then King Abyasa states that he wishes to meditate in order to seek insight as to what course of action he should follow at this moment when Ngastina's fate appears to hang in the balance.

They retire, at which point two female servants appear. One is old and of slight stature, while the other is very large and deep-voiced. The contrast between their appearance and that of the queens who have just left could not be greater. Where the queens were of delicate proportions and fine features, these maidservants have unrefined and unattractive looks. As with all shadow puppets, their physical appearance corresponds to their temperament: refined characters, like the queens, have elegantly long noses, narrow eyes, and tiny figures (Plate 11), whereas these low-status women are, in a word, frumpy. And just as appearance reflects character (Plates 12 and 13), so does speech. Ki Anom speaks for these maidservants in a feminine manner, as he did for the queens just before, but these characters speak in a coarse and humorous style that contrasts with the queens' softly pronounced and respectfully phrased speech. The Javanese language is very elaborately graded for the degree of refinement one shows in one's speech, and the choices one makes among speaking styles reflect both one's own temperament and one's status relative to the person one is addressing. Queens address their royal husband in the highest reaches of respectful Javanese; maidservants address each other in an everyday, frank, and even uncouth style befitting their status. However, when speaking to their mistress, maidservants would attempt a more refined mode, while a queen would address them in a matter-of-fact and unadorned fashion. A *dalang* must adjust the manner in which he impersonates each character's speech in accordance with this intense Javanese concern with social standing and its reflection in speech.

The older of the two maidservants mentions that she is going to Mr Sastradimeja's house, to take part in a celebration of the good fortune he and his wife have enjoyed in their business dealings, a celebration conceived as a way of giving thanks to the spirits that watch over the area where they live. These remarks, put in the mouth of one of the maidservants, are really a way of informing the audience of who has invited Ki Anom to come and perform and why. Many shadow plays are performed in Java at the request of families who are celebrating some ritual occasion, and a *dalang* will often introduce references to the nature of the event into the speech of one or another of the comic, lower-status characters. The two servants go on to talk about just how good the food may be that guests at the event will be served: here the audience begins to enjoy the way

PANDHU CROWNED KING

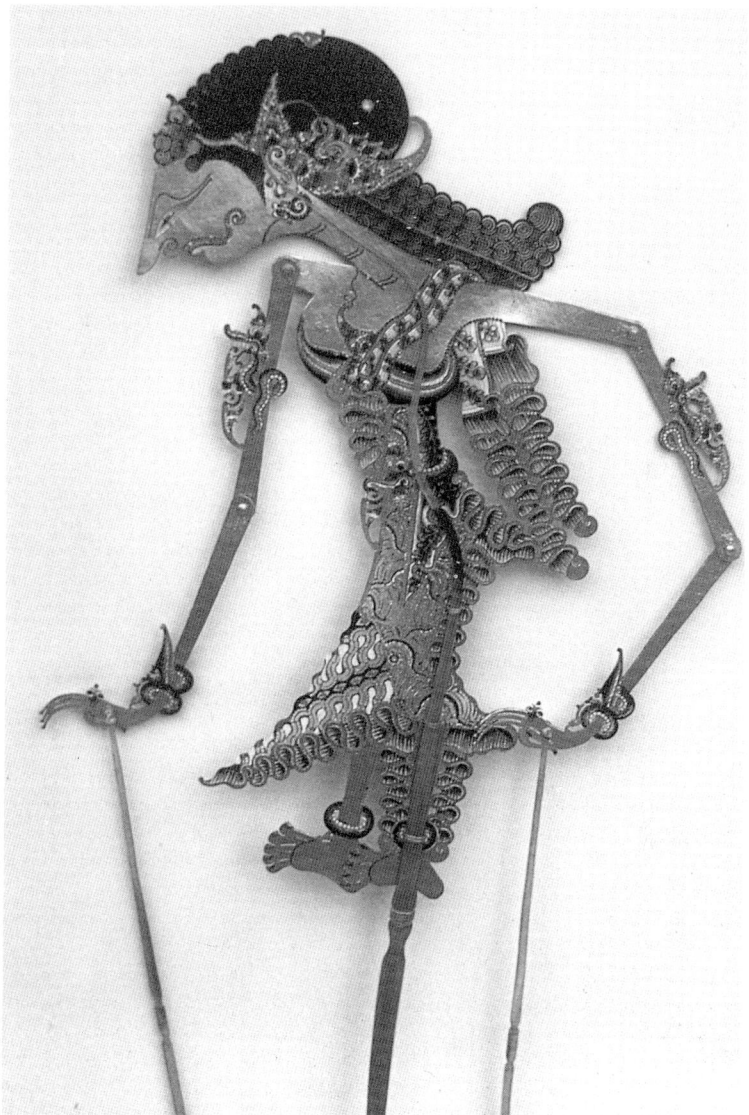

11. A princess's refinement and modesty can be seen in her tiny dimensions and downcast gaze. (Jacques Dumarçay)

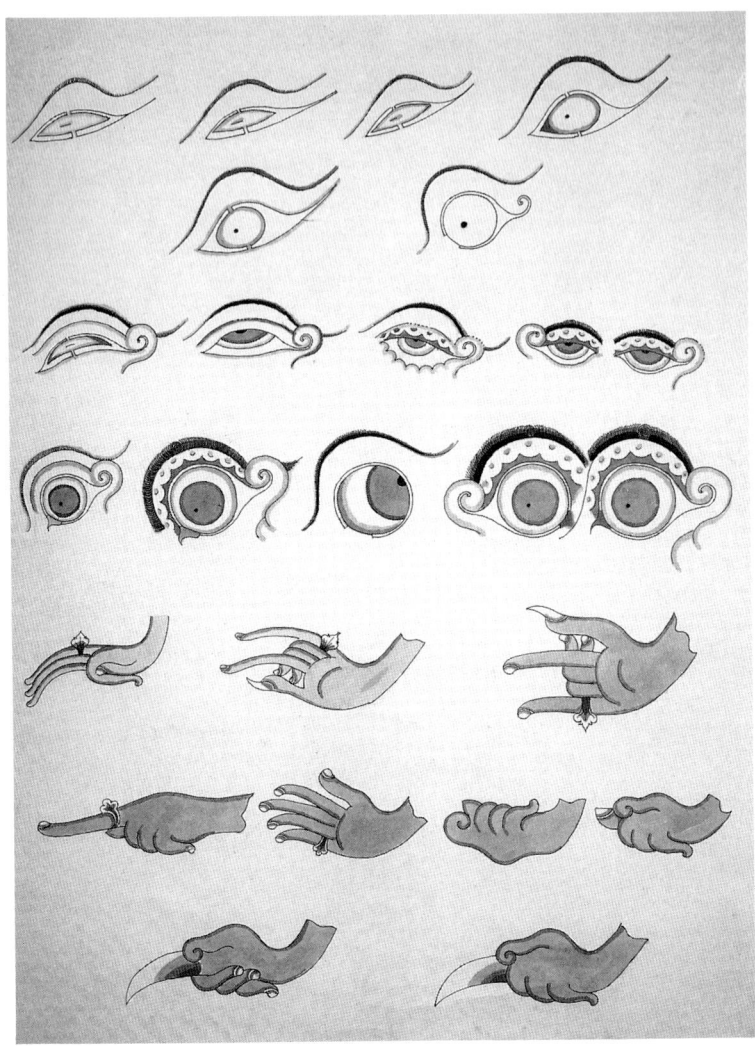

12. Convention governs the appearance of every part of a puppet's body. Illustrated here is a range of eye and hand shapes. (Drawing by Suharso)

PANDHU CROWNED KING

13. The angle of a figure's head indicates temperament. A downcast gaze indicates humility; a straight gaze indicates bravery or brazenness. (Drawing by Suharso)

Ki Anom is teasing his hosts. They then gossip about which of the *gamelan* players the very large and plain younger maidservant might entice into marriage. At this point, members of Ki Anom's troupe break into loud guffaws.

Following this amusing scene, King Kunthiboja reappears on the screen, joined by a number of knightly figures. These are the knights who have accompanied him from Madura, and among them is his son, Basudéwa. Kunthiboja explains to him that it is thanks to Abyasa's good offices that Madura has been made a kingdom separate from Ngastina, of which it used to be a part, and that Kunthiboja was named its king. Therefore, Kunthiboja and his kin and followers must be willing to defend Abyasa and his realm at all costs. They will now advance to battle.

This discussion introduces one of the set pieces included in all performances of *wayang*, the departure of the troops. Ki Anom cues the orchestra to begin playing a light, rhythmic piece and then portrays the knights as they set out for battle, each one displaying an idiosyncratic gait. The story is not advanced by this scene, but Ki Anom uses it as an opportunity to display his technical virtuosity and originality at manipulating the many puppets.

The only moving parts of most figures are their arms, which are jointed at the shoulders and elbows. Some characters, such as some of the ogres that appear later, have only one arm that moves, and others have no joints at all (Plates 14 and 15). Yet, the lack of movable parts does not make manipulating the puppets easy: a skilled puppeteer has spent countless hours learning how to hold a puppet's central stem and to move it in a variety of ways in order to suggest a great range of gestures. Indeed, although shadow puppets lack the moving legs, rotating necks, or blinking eyes that are given puppets in other traditions in an effort to enliven them, *wayang* appear anything but lifeless in performance. Improbable though it may seem, the highly stylized figures and their conventional movements come to seem not just familiar but even 'natural' to the spectator accustomed to seeing them. In the course of a performance,

14. The Lord Guru, or Siva, is the highest god to appear in most performances. He boasts four arms, but the figure has no moving parts. (Drawing by Suharso)

15. A knight from the human world, centre, has an interview with the Lord Guru, at right, and his prime minister, Narada, in heaven. Both of the knight's arms move, but only one of Narada's, and neither of Lord Guru's. (Leslie Morris)

one starts before long to imagine expressions of malice, rage, sly humour, or dumbfounded surprise crossing the faces of the characters, so convincing does this completely unrealistic genre become.

Ki Anom now refers to another court, this one in the kingdom of Ngalengkapura. By means of a verbal pun he cues the *gamelan* orchestra to play another stately musical piece, against which he describes the scene. We now observe the large and coarse-looking King Wisamuka in consultation with his counsellors as he reflects upon the challenge he has addressed to Pandhu and the kingdom of Ngastina. A lesser official, mis-shapen and ungainly looking, argues against the king's aggression. It is true, he explains, that Pandhu killed Wisamuka's father. But the latter, Nagakilat, had challenged the gods, demanding eternal life for himself, and they had turned to Pandhu, even though he was only an infant, for assistance in defeating him. Pandhu had been born in a caul. The gods told Nagakilat that he could obtain eternal life if he could break open the caul. Nagakilat did so, but went on to bludgeon the baby, who grew only larger with each of Nagakilat's blows and finally killed his attacker. Death, the official advising King Wisamuka concludes, is the reward to be reaped by anyone who, like his father, challenges the gods. But Wisamuka is not at all daunted, and his sister, Wisawati, suggests that she could avenge their father's death and murder Pandhu by means of her irresistible beauty. Her brother approves the plan and they set out for Ngastina.

The troops that left Ngastina under Kunthiboja's command now meet up with ogres in the forest. Combat in shadow plays is always one on one: a figure who fails to triumph over his opponent may yield his place to another, more powerful ally, but the knightly code will not permit them to attack another character in concert. The victor from each match, meanwhile, goes on to meet a new challenger until he is defeated. This system, similar to play-offs, applies to fights even with ogres, but such contests are played for comedy: ogres are too stupid and coarse to present a real threat to knights.

When Kunthiboja's troops encounter the ones from Ngalengkapura, the battles become more serious. King Wisamuka's younger brother engages Kunthiboja's younger son, Ugraséna, in battle, but the former fares badly. In this instance it is a woman who replaces Wisamuka's vanquished brother: his sister, the lovely Wisawati. Her presence startles Ugraséna and soon enchants him: he asks that she marry him and she agrees. But when she touches his hand, he becomes powerless and she tells her brother to imprison him. She then repeats this ploy with Basudéwa, and yet again with the two brothers' father, Kunthiboja himself. The only one among Ngastina's defenders who sees the nature of the danger and withdraws is Mandradipa, who takes the remaining troops with him. This skirmish has ended, as the first battle of every *wayang* always ends, in a stand-off.

The scene now shifts to Seven Peaks, the hermitage where Pandhu is doing ascetic exercises accompanied by four menservants. There is no scenery in a shadow play, only the two or three large *kayon*, resembling inverted cones, that the *dalang* uses as all-purpose props. So it is left to spectators listening to Ki Anom's narration to imagine how this mountain hermitage appears. But before bringing the puppets on, Ki Anom places one *kayon* before the screen. He has done this at the beginning of earlier scenes, but this time, rather than inclining it to one side as he has been doing, he stands it straight up. He thereby signals the transition to the middle part of the performance.

The shift entails a change in musical mode (*pathet*). The Javanese *gamelan* can be played in three different scales, differing so much that they must be played on different sets of instruments. Within two of those scales, there are different modes, distinguished by which notes in the scale receive the most stress at the ends of musical phrases. Shadow plays have traditionally been performed in only one of the scales, called *sléndro*. Every performance is divided up into three parts, each marked by the use of a different mode. Each mode tends to emphasize a slightly higher range than the preceding one, and this means that a *dalang*, like the unfortunate tenor in Wagner's *Siegfried*, must reach for ever higher notes even as his voice tires in the course of a performance. A fortunate few *dalang*, including Ki Anom, rarely exhibit any strain in their voices, despite the great demands that singing the long phrases of poetry that punctuate every scene places on their vocal cords.

It is not until this second section of a *wayang* that the menservants to the virtuous party appear. They are an older, obese figure named Semar and his three adoptive sons, Pétruk, Nala Garèng, and Bagong (Colour Plate 12). Javanese dearly love these characters and know their traits and voices as well as Westerners know Charlie Chaplin's gait or Buster Keaton's consistently deadpan persona. They invariably engage in horse-play and joking, and sing light, popular songs of the day, some of them to satisfy the requests of members of the audience who pass notes to the *dalang* to communicate their wishes. The tall and scrawny Pétruk often appears first, and he serves as something of a mouthpiece for the *dalang*, who may choose Pétruk's opening comments as the best place in which to insert references to government programmes that officials wish *dalang* to communicate to their audiences. Although these comments may start out in a serious tone, Pétruk soon joins in the play of jibes and tricks that mark his dealings with his brothers and father. (Official pressure to promote family planning, for example, affords a chance for many racy jokes.) A light, diffuse atmosphere then prevails for up to an hour. For the rest of the performance, the four figures will provide comic moments, sometimes side-splittingly funny ones, as they engage in mock-heroic battles with their masters' enemies, and they will highlight the courtly code of honour of their superiors by means of their contrastingly mundane and unheroic words and deeds.

Semar reminds his sons that they should attend to the needs of their master, Pandhu, who wears such a mantle of sorrow that he will address no one. Only after much effort do they persuade Pandhu to speak. He explains that he has received a divine sign that he is soon to be made king of Ngastina but he feels inadequate to the task and is praying to the Lord to assist him. Semar approves Pandhu's decision to make this request here, since it is the spot at which Pandhu's forefathers before him obtained divine boons, and to do ascetic exercises here is not to pray to rocks and trees but rather to appeal to the spirits of his ancestors for guidance.

Their conversation is interrupted when a wild buffalo enters and wreaks havoc in the hermitage. It succumbs to Pandhu's arrow and is transformed into a large, powerful warrior named Jaka Abilawa who thanks Pandhu for releasing him—by defeating him in combat—from a curse he had suffered for trying to seduce another man's wife. Pandhu accepts his request to become his follower and sends him to greet his father, King Abyasa, and inform him that he, Abilawa, will be the commander of the troops when Pandhu assumes the throne. Next an elephant enters and another of Pandhu's arrows reveals Bayu, the god of the winds, who has also suffered a curse: he was punished for blowing high the skirts of the nymphs of heaven! Bayu takes Pandhu as his adopted son and gives him a weapon to bequeath to some future child, but on the condition that that child be of a strength and stature equal to Bayu's own. Then a tiger enters and is killed by another of Pandhu's arrows. The tiger lies dead, to the anguished cries of a wild boar that comes upon its body. But the boar is killed in turn. The tiger and boar turn out to be the god of love, Kamajaya, and his wife, the nymph Ratih. They announce that they have been instructed by Lord Guru, the god of heaven, to give Pandhu a boon in recognition of his long ascetic rigours, namely, a weapon with which he will be able to subjugate all sprites and evil spirits. He should rest assured, as well, that he will reign as king of Ngastina. As they withdraw to heaven, Pandhu expresses his pleasure at having been given such bounty from the gods. He will now leave the hermitage.

Ki Anom, directing the *gamelan* to play another stately composition, puts aside the story-line developed so far and begins to describe yet another kingdom across the sea, the 'Land above the winds', in India. Like Abyasa, the king of this realm, King Baratmeja, has two sons and wishes to relinquish the throne to one of them. The chosen son, Sucitra, is unwilling to accept such responsibilities, however, even after his father tells him that his brother is not capable of taking the crown because he is trained only in the ways of spirituality, not of rule. King Baratmeja is exasperated by his son's continued recalcitrance, and when Sucitra tells his father that he should kill him rather than make him king, King Baratmeja in a rage makes as if to do just that. As his father lunges to attack him with his sword, however, Sucitra flees, pursued by his brother, Kumbayana, who urges both his father and his brother to restrain themselves. But Sucitra will have none of it, and eventually Kumbayana, too, loses his patience and they fight. They are equally matched and neither one prevails until Kumbayana finally uses a very powerful arrow in his possession. It proves effective, but rather than kill Sucitra, it causes him to be knocked across the sea, to Java. Kumbayana, distraught at what he has done, calls out sorrowfully to his brother, assuring him that he will follow him to that far off island.

By now it is about three in the morning. A spectator sitting or standing outside is likely to have grown sleepy, especially during this preceding scene, in which there were no servants to provide the laughs that help keep people attentive as the performance goes on into the small hours. Some spectators have already got up and gone home. The story is unusually interesting, however, and Ki Anom is so adept at making it entertaining that a much larger crowd than usual continues to fight off sleep and the chill night air, trying to see it through to the denouement. To keep oneself going and warm oneself up, someone might well stand up, stretch, and stroll a bit.

At the edges of the crowd, a few clusters of men squat near kerosene lamps. They are gambling for small stakes. People are selling cigarettes in little packs: it is standard to buy the clove-scented or incense-scented cigarettes Indonesian men smoke avidly in packs of ten or twelve, but it is also possible to buy them singly if buying ten at once is beyond someone's means. There are little toys for sale, too, especially little cardboard imitation shadow puppets to give children. And some pedicabs are parked at the edge of the crowd, their operators sitting or sleeping in the seats, maybe hoping someone will tire of the performance and need a ride, maybe just finding an enjoyable way to pass the time till morning. Interspersed among them are snack-sellers who have set out tables with food and benches to sit on. The tables are covered with trays of snacks, plus glass jars, modelled after Dutch containers, crammed with fried peanut crackers flavoured with garlic and shallots, ginger-peanut candies, and other snacks people can munch on as they drink glasses of sweet coffee or jasmine-flavoured tea. One or two women stand next to great plaited bamboo baskets filled with rice, which they will serve with a bit of broth and soybean cakes or maybe a piece of fried meat to those wanting a heartier meal. A few men have set large metal containers over flames to warm a sweet, gingery liquid they will ladle into small bowls with dumplings for customers, a tangy and warming refreshment popular especially now, as the air gets cold (Plate 16).

These sellers, their customers, and the gamblers and pedicabs form a large, irregular U around the crowd of people still gathered to watch the performance. Some of them talk, but most keep one ear cocked, listening for the gist of what the *dalang* is saying as his voice booms through the loudspeaker. Ki Anom, like most puppeteers, has no trouble differentiating voices enough to assure that once one knows who is present in a scene one can tell who is speaking without needing to look at the screen. Indeed, the voices of several important figures, including of course the ever-popular servants, are instantly recognizable to most Javanese without need of any identification. So one can sit and enjoy a hot glass of rich, black Javanese coffee, spitting out a few grounds that fail to settle to the bottom or gulping them down as one wishes, without losing track of what is going on.

Ki Anom introduces another scene, to the accompaniment of a composition in one of the two *pélog* scales. This is a scale not traditionally used in shadow plays, but if the people that ask a puppeteer to perform have the means to rent a complete

16. Casual spectators can stave off hunger pangs and the chill night air at little stalls on the perimeter of the performance area, where meatball soup (*bakso*), tea and coffee, and a variety of snacks are available. (Drawing by Suharso)

orchestra, not just those instruments that play the basic, *sléndro* scale, he will include a few pieces in the *pélog* scales. These are scales non-Javanese often find particularly attractive, and there is something especially enjoyable about this musical interlude in the depths of the night, as the women vocalists sing long, sinuous phrases in subtle rhythmic play with the steady beat of the ensemble. The mood, as most of the world sleeps, is what Javanese term *sarèh*: deeply, almost meditatively, tranquil, a state many Javanese idealize.

Comedy soon returns, however, to enliven the atmosphere. The scene is in a village, where an old man, the Venerable Dhudhu Wangkung, who is 130 years old, lives with his twenty-five-year-old wife, Nikèn Tapi. Dhudhu Wangkung praises his wife for her loyalty but still expresses some worry as to whether she feels truly committed to attending to his needs. She protests that he need harbour no such doubts: after all, had she not been so devoted to him, she would have gone off with Jaka Abilawa when he urged her to do so. (The audience realizes that this is the woman for whom Abilawa had lusted and been cursed to become a wild bull, although Ki Anom does not make the connection explicitly.) Dhudhu Wangkung is still anxious: since he cannot be a man for her, as he rather delicately puts it, can she really accept things as they are? What must fit are only our feelings, Nikèn Tapi replies, expressing an oft-repeated Javanese remark about human relationships but one that takes on a slightly blue hue in this context. Dhudhu Wangkung laughs with pleasure at this comforting rejoinder, laughter that makes him cough—and then fart. The audience roars, and several of the musicians, who are nodding off over their instruments, start and join in the laughter. A *dalang* will use some jokes many times over, to the point that musicians that accompany him often will no longer laugh at them. But a *dalang* with a talent for comedy will come up with many new jokes on the spot, in performance, and these will evoke the musicians' mirth, helping to keep them awake until dawn—or at least close enough to consciousness to snap to when the music starts.

This model couple's conversation is interrupted when two thieves enter their home and demand the old man's wealth and livestock. The dutiful Nikèn Tapi tries to save her husband by picking him up and running, but the thieves catch them. When she finds her husband again, now lying on the ground, he moans that they have taken his most valuable possession, an arrow called 'One grain of rice', that enabled him to feed anyone in want of food. They must seek allies to help them regain the arrow. The thieves, meanwhile, gloat over their ill-gotten goods, but soon fight over who will have possession of the magic arrow.

Nikèn Tapi and her ancient husband chance upon Pandhu and his servants. Two of the latter, Pétruk and Bagong, cannot contain their astonishment that such an unlikely pair are married. Bagong, who speaks in a way that makes him sound dull-witted but who often speaks the truth, remarks that it is like a man marrying his niece. At this, the musicians all break up, laughing and hooting derisively. The audience sits in silence, unaware of what was so funny. They can only assume that Ki Anom has made a veiled reference to the personal affairs of one of his players. Such asides, making a comment that purports to be about one thing but alludes unmistakably to something else, is called 'throwing north and hitting south' in Javanese and is a highly prized form of humour.

Pandhu promises to assist Dhudhu Wangkung and Nikèn Tapi and uses a magic formula that draws the two thieves—still fighting—to him. Pétruk hits them, but Bagong upbraids him for this, telling him that he is not a judge and therefore has no right to exact punishment: this is a nation of law, and people cannot take justice into their own hands. Here, Ki Anom is seconding a government effort to persuade Indonesian citizens that they must rely on the legal system to punish criminals. In the past, thieves caught in a village were often beaten to death, and the Indonesian government insists that that practice must be abandoned.

The thieves admit their crime, and after listening to words of wisdom from Pandhu, and more vigorous criticism from the servants, they proclaim themselves cured of their criminal habit. Pandhu promises them posts as members of his army following his accession to the kingship and tells them to precede him to Ngastina. Pandhu then gives the recovered magic arrow to Dhudhu Wangkung, who gives it back again: it is the reward for Pandhu's assistance, for him to use on behalf of any of his subjects in want of food.

The village couple leave Pandhu, and now Sucitra appears, saying that he is looking for the king of Ngastina, to whom he wishes to offer his allegiance. Pandhu tells him that the king is Abyasa, his father, and that he accepts Sucitra as his kinsman, inviting him to accompany him on his journey to the kingdom. Then Gandamana, the prospective prime minister of Ngastina whom we have not seen since the opening scene, appears, telling Pandhu of his father's plan to withdraw to Seven Peaks and of King Wisamuka's challenge to Pandhu to fight. They all set out for Ngastina.

Along the way they must do battle with a number of ogres, monsters, and creatures that make progress through the unpeopled expanses of *wayang*'s mythic landscape treacherous. These encounters, accompanied by a pounding, repetitive series of short musical phrases, display Ki Anom's dexterity and, once again, his humour, particularly as the servants come forward to join battles of wits as well as strength with a variety of large brutes. Only after much travail, and many funny escapades, does the company of warriors and servants reach their destination.

In Ngastina, Mandradipa informs Abyasa of the manner in which so many knights have fallen prey to Wisawati, seduced by her allure and then imprisoned. Abyasa's son still at court, Drestarata, wishes to advance directly into battle, but his father restrains him. Pandhu and his entourage arrive at this moment. When Abyasa learns of Sucitra's intention to serve him, he sends him to fight Wisamuka as the test of his prowess and commitment. Sucitra goes with the servants to the prison where the four knights are being held. Sucitra uses a magic formula to destroy the prison, releasing its hostages. They then all proceed to King Wisamuka's encampment. Sucitra himself falls prey to Wisawati's ploys, but Semar rescues him and then battles the seductress. Suddenly, she is turned into a post. Sucitra then fights King Wisamuka himself, who suffers the same fate. Pandhu enters, explaining that in both instances he shot the arrow given him by the gods, and that Sucitra has been accepted as his kinsman.

When they return to court, Abyasa gives Pandhu clothes for his coronation. Ki Anom takes the two puppets off the screen and replaces them with two others: these are Pandhu in the crown and rich ornaments of a king and Abyasa in the simple robe of a forest sage. Abyasa announces that he will now retire to Seven Peaks, Sucitra is now Pandhu's younger brother, Gandamana is now the prime minister of Ngastina, and Pandhu's coronation will now take place.

Ki Anom places one of the *kayon* in the middle of the screen, and the orchestra falls silent. The stillness, after so many hours of unceasing sound, is eerie. Birds can be heard twittering, and one or two motor bikes starting up. There is a dim half-light, in which the musicians and Ki Anom can be seen standing up and stretching. The performance is over.

2
Wayang in Javanese Society

THE story related in the course of an eight-hour long shadow play may be quite complicated, as the many different scenes and characters in 'Pandhu Crowned King' demonstrate. But untangling the various characters and turns in the plot of a performance does not exhaust the complexity of the event. Another kind of complexity about a *wayang kulit* performance lies in its social complexity, the many ways people are brought together in preparing, executing, and even recollecting the performance. It is worth taking up the performance of 'Pandhu Crowned King' described in the preceding chapter once again to fill in some of this social depth, thereby adding an essential dimension.

Just before and during the opening scene of the performance, a great many people converge on the house where the play is being held. A majority of them join the many others milling about in front of the house, but a few of them proceed inside the house, shaking hands with a number of men lining their path as they do so. These men entering the house are invited guests of the sponsoring family, the family that has commissioned Ki Anom and his troupe to perform. Many of the guests wear what might be termed Javanese semi-formal attire: a suit jacket over a white shirt, either a batiked or a machine-woven skirt, and a black velvet cap. One or two of the men greeting the guests are dressed, like Ki Anom, in full Javanese dress: a batik skirt with pleats down the front and a long sash wrapped several times around the waist, a plain shirt, and a double-breasted Javanese court jacket, plus a Javanese dagger at the back and a batiked cap. These, the most important men among those greeting the guests, are close relatives of the sponsoring family. Once the guests have been greeted and have gone inside, they are seated, usually (in the Solonese region) on metal chairs set out in rows in the inner part of the house, or (in the Jogjanese region) on mats. (In Plate 6 men can be seen sitting on metal chairs behind the screen, whereas in Plate 17 they can be seen sitting on mats.)

Some guests arrive on motor bikes. They make their way slowly through the crowd to an area off to one side of the house where young men take the motor bike and give its owner a numbered check with which to reclaim it later. These young men are neighbourhood youths, a few among the many people donating their labour to the sponsoring family. They are dressed in dark slacks, white shirts, and ties that clip on at the collar. Some of the guests wear slacks and a shirt, too; several of them wear elaborately batiked shirts that are the mark of the wealthy new Javanese bourgeoisie. After parking and locking their motor bikes, these men, too, make their way inside the house.

Only a few women accompany their husbands to the *wayang*. Those that do come wear formal Javanese women's attire: a long batik skirt tightly wrapped around the legs, a lacey, close-fitting blouse over a dark bodice, and a large hairpiece at the back of the head, plus as much jewellery as they own or can borrow for the occasion. These ladies go with their husbands only as far as the entrance to the house, whereupon they leave them and go toward the inner part of the house to join other women, both guests and assistants to the sponsors. If they watch any part of the performance, they will do so from within the interior of the house. Women do not usually think it appropriate to be seen staying up till all hours watching a shadow play performance.

Once the play is well under way—by the time Abyasa has returned to his chambers and the queens' maidservants are conversing casually with each other—the guests sitting behind the screen are served snacks. This performance is being given near Klaten, in the Solonese region, and as is customary in that area a pair of young people do the serving: a young man in Western clothes carries a tray filled with glasses of sweet tea and slices of cake, and a young woman in Javanese dress serves them to each guest. In Jogja, young men do the serving. Rather

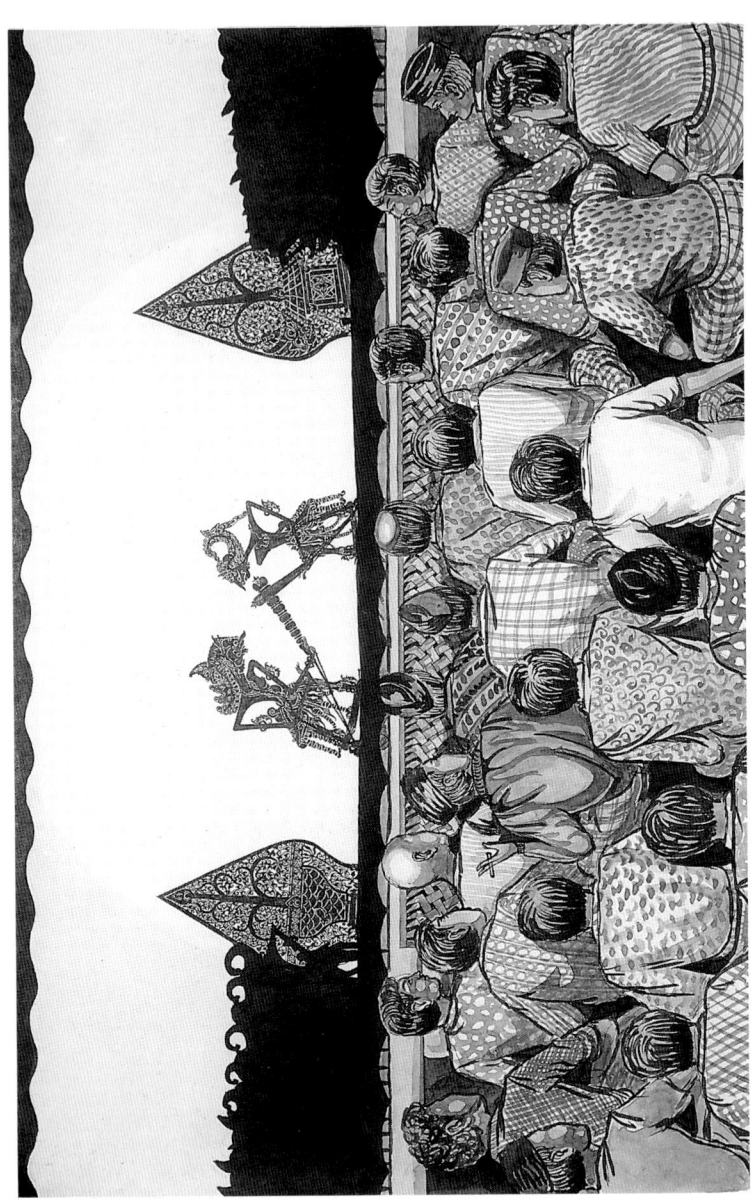

17. Early in a performance, many guests who have received formal invitations watch the performance from the shadow side of the screen. Here they are shown sitting on mats on the floor, a practice that is now more common in the Jogjanese area than in the Solonese. (Drawing by Suharso)

1. This knight's refinement, and his servant, Nala Gareng's lack of it, illustrate the contrasts in *wayang*'s stylized iconography.

2. Two princesses do battle in this Jogjanese performance of *wayang wong*, a genre in which humans impersonate characters from the shadow plays and even imitate many of their gestures. (Edward Frey)

3. A hunting scene painted on glass. (Jacques Dumarçay)

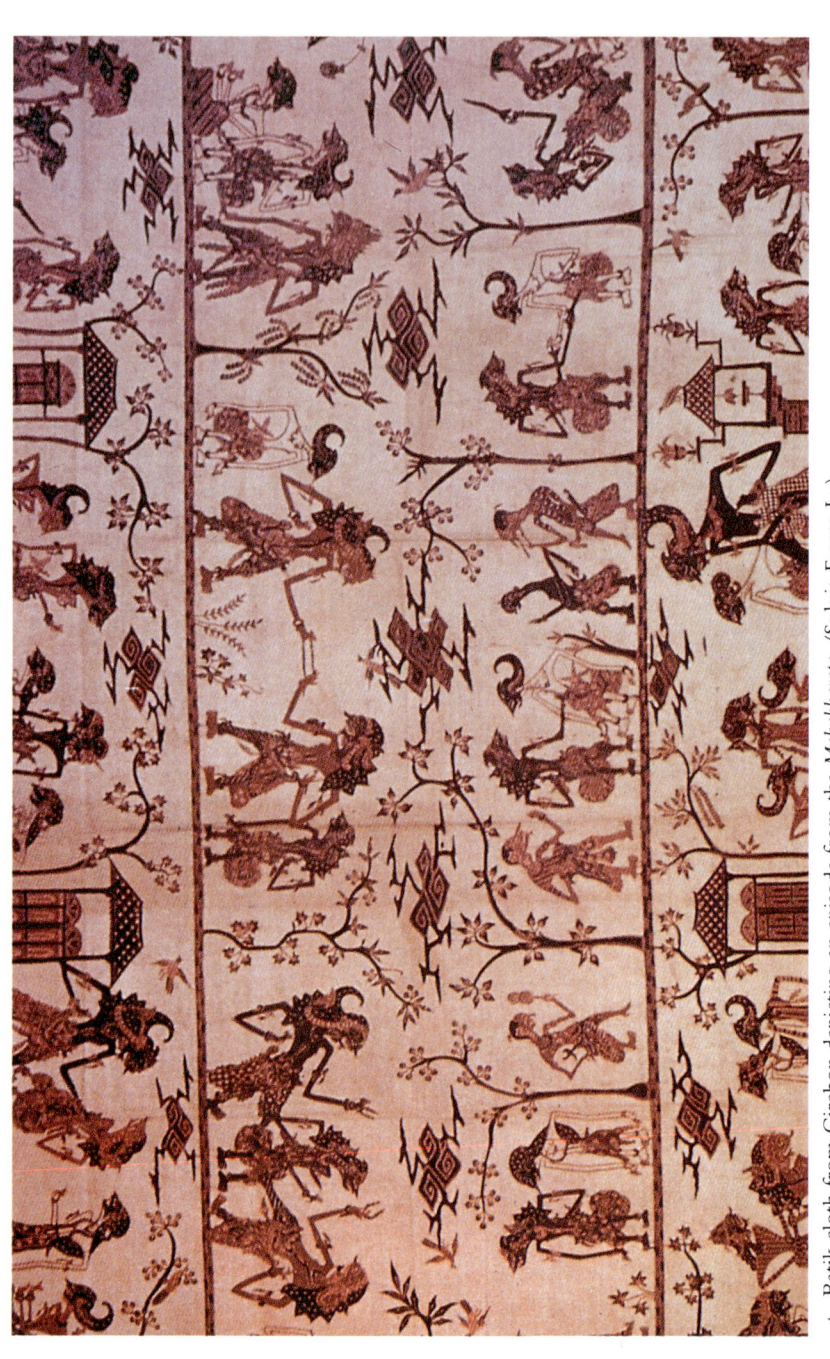

4. Batik cloth from Cirebon depicting an episode from the *Mahabharata*. (Sylvia Fraser-Lu)

5. The performing space actually takes up only a small part of the screen. Dozens of other puppets are lined up in front of the rest of the screen, to either side of the puppeteer. (Leslie Morris)

6. The man playing the *gender* sits closest to the *dalang*, providing him with a soft, velvety accompaniment as he speaks and sings throughout the night. (Leslie Morris)

7. The *dalang* grasps thin sticks made out of buffalo horn to manipulate each figure's arms. A thicker central stem can be planted in the banana tree-trunk below the screen when the figure is stationary, or grasped, as here, to make the whole figure move.

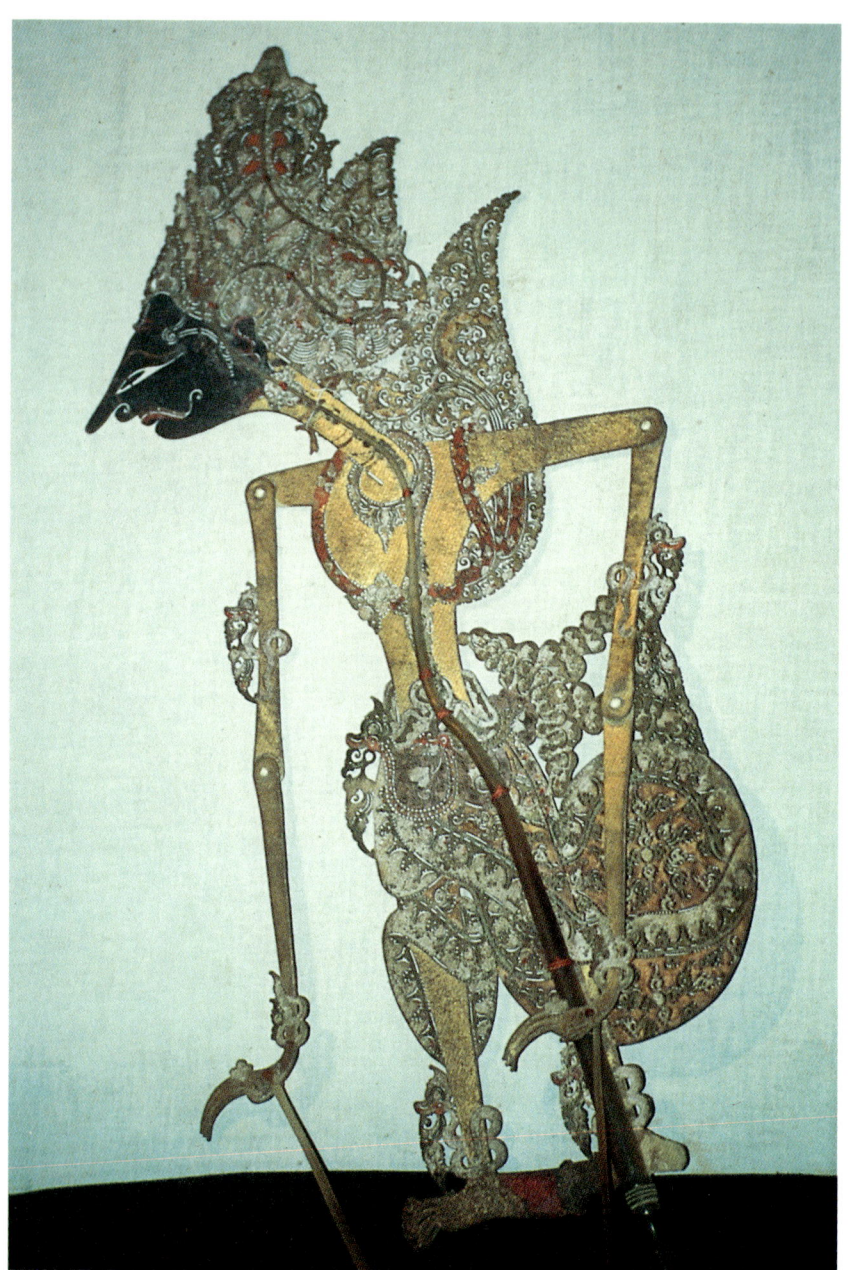

8. Like most puppets, the elegant and imposing Kresna is jointed only at each shoulder and elbow. Nevertheless, a good *dalang* can impart a remarkable range of movements and gestures to each figure.

9. The delicacy and subtlety of the images cast upon the screen is truly remarkable. (Judith Ferster)

10. The high status of kings is observed in the way the puppeteer places the central stem of a king's puppet in the higher of the two banana tree-trunk supports. The lower status of his ladies-in-waiting is evident in the way they are secured in the lower banana tree-trunk. (Leslie Morris)

11. The women sitting in the front row sing the long, sinuous lines of Javanese vocal music singly, the men behind them in unison, in the course of a performance. (Judith Ferster)

12. One of the best-loved *wayang* figures, the servant Nala Garèng, is cross-eyed, has a pot belly, and a club foot. In Jogja he has a high, squeaky voice, in Solo a deep one.

13. A woman assists the sponsors of a performance by tending to rice steaming over a fire. Many such quantities of rice will be consumed in the course of a ritual celebration, served to guests, performers, and the sponsors' volunteer assistants. (Leslie Morris)

14. Before and after guests are served rice, they are urged to nibble on a variety of sweets, bananas, and other goodies. Here, plates of such snacks are readied. Young people will soon pick them up and distribute them among the guests.

15. Neighbourhood youths and boys crowd around the platform behind the orchestra during a daytime performance.

16. Bima, painted on paper. (Jacques Dumarçay)

than walk among guests seated on the floor, which would be an affront to their elders' status, the young men must practise an elaborate movement—called 'kneeling walking'—in which they hold trays level with their heads while walking in a crouching position. Later, by eleven or midnight, these young people will return to refill people's glasses and to serve each of them a plate of rice plus side dishes. (If the sponsors are very well-to-do, they may increase the number of courses, possibly including a soup course before the rice, and/or dessert. Particularly dramatic is to serve a little cup of ice-cream, since refrigeration is not yet widespread in Java, especially in villages.)

After they have finished their meal, the invited guests sitting behind the screen remain a little while, watching the antics of the servants attending Pandhu at the hermitage of Seven Peaks. But they soon leave, filing out in a long line as the same men who welcomed them now bid them goodbye. By this time it is midnight or one in the morning, and youths and young boys stream into the area behind the screen that the guests have vacated. Most of them soon fall asleep, but they wake up for the battles with ogres, a part of the performance they greatly enjoy, and for the battles that take up much of the last part of the performance (Plate 18). A few of their elders have enjoyed the first part of Ki Anom's performance so much that they would prefer not to go home just yet. But they are reluctant to stay on inside, where the sponsors would still feel obliged to serve them more food and tea, and so they go outside and mix anonymously in the crowd.

This performance is being given by a wealthy family whose business ventures have done well, especially in the production and sale of elaborately carved teak and rattan furniture to urban dwellers. As Ki Anom has hinted in an earlier scene, they wish to express their gratitude to God, to the spirit of the vicinity, and to the spirits of their ancestors in granting them such prosperity. In providing an entertainment that will attract a great many people, both guests and casual spectators, they will also win the thanks of a multitude of people and give their own prestige a great boost.

18. Long past midnight, the invited guests have gone home, and younger males have come in to watch the shadows. Some of them engage in horseplay, while others stretch out for a sleep until the battles near the end of the performance wake them up. (Drawing by Suharso)

Since long before Ki Anom sat down in front of the screen and started the performance, the sponsors have been overseeing the arrangements, checking the food supplies, greeting their guests, and receiving contributions from them to help defray their expenses. (They must carefully commit the amounts of these contributions to memory, so that they can reciprocate appropriately at a later date.) They have been doing all this for days, they have had very little sleep, and they are exhausted.

Javanese think that going without sleep is beneficial to one's well-being; they view it as a form of self-sacrifice that will win God's favour, and they do not think it inappropriate that sponsors confronting an important event like this one should undertake such an ascetic exercise. After all, everyone involved in such an event stands at risk of attack from evil forces abroad in the world. Ascetic rigours of any sort are a means to stave off those forces' attacks. Many sponsors, however, collapse into an exhausted sleep long before a *wayang* ends, and must be roused at its completion in order to pay the puppeteer and say farewell to him and his troupe. Nevertheless, while they have been both too busy and too exhausted to enjoy the performance they have made possible, the sponsors are happy. They know that they will long be remembered as the family that engaged Ki Anom Soeroto to perform.

Not all *wayang* are performed at the behest of families. In general, sponsors fall into three categories: families observing life-passage rituals, communities observing community-wide ritual occasions, usually on an annual basis, and institutions, most often government ones, marking some important event, such as the anniversary of its founding or the opening of a new building.

Families sponsor shadow play performances to celebrate any of a number of events in their lives. A daughter's wedding is the event most likely to be put on with the greatest display a family can manage, and a *wayang* is considered by many Javanese to be the grandest display of all. A son's circumcision, which takes place anywhere from the age of eight to fourteen or so, may be marked with a *wayang*, as can a woman's first pregnancy ritual, the ritual on the thirty-fifth day following the birth of a child, or the final funerary ritual that occurs 1,000 days after a person's death.

These and other life-passage rituals can all be observed very modestly, in which case the family invites only a few close kin and friends. They would put on no entertainment, let alone a large-scale one like a *wayang*. But if they wish to make something of the event—and most people wish to do so if their finances permit—then they mount a large social gathering called *nduwé gawé*, literally, 'to have work'. This means sending out invitations to hundreds of people, and marshalling many kinspeople and neighbours, who contribute both labour and foodstuffs in order to entertain and feed those guests. Men work on setting up the house. If it is an old-style Javanese house with a row of doors across the front, they remove these to create a large space opening out to the front yard in which to accommodate guests. Women, meanwhile, cook huge quantities of rice and side dishes to serve the many guests and volunteer labourers that gather in the course of the event (Colour Plates 13 and 14).

All of this activity goes on for a day, or even several days, before the main ritual event, such as the meeting of bride and groom or a son's circumcision. Over that same time, couples come to give the family monetary contributions and they are given snacks and a meal as well as the sponsors' formal greetings. Or they may come and make their contributions on the day of the event. In any case, people who have made contributions are welcome to attend the event itself, often sitting in straight, hard-backed chairs for long periods while high-status guests of the sponsors give speeches. Weddings are particularly liable to prove long and dull, but any event may elicit copious amounts of talk from those people asked to do the sponsors the honour of addressing the assembled guests.

A *wayang*, when held in connection with these events, becomes a part of the crowded, noisy, enjoyable atmosphere that sponsors hope to assure at such times. It should draw a large number of guests, something that helps to keep potentially bothersome spirits at bay, and at the same time reflects well on the status of the sponsors in the human world. The sponsors may even put on two performances: one during the day, for the benefit of guests come to make their contributions, and then the performance held at night, which is the main event. A daytime performance does not keep anyone's attention, except for some neighbourhood children's, for very long, and the *dalang* who will be performing at night usually has a relative take his place during the day (Colour Plate 15).

How many people come to watch a night-time performance depends, of course, on the fame and popularity of the puppeteer the sponsors hire. A local puppeteer who performs often in the area may not draw much of a crowd, although there will always be some people interested in coming to see at least the first few scenes of a performance. By inviting Ki Anom Soeroto to perform, the sponsors of the performance described above guaranteed that a great crowd would gather, and proved—since they could lay out the funds necessary to pay Ki Anom's large fee, and to feed all those guests—that they were doing very well for themselves indeed.

Private families probably sponsor a majority of performances in Java today, but it may not always have been so. In the past, most villagers probably saw shadow plays primarily in the context of annual village rituals. Many hamlets in Java traditionally celebrated—and many still do—an annual ritual to protect the area from misfortune and the depredations of malevolent spirits. Sometimes this is linked to procedures marking the harvesting of rice; sometimes the two events are observed on different occasions. Either event, village purification (*bersih désa*) or harvest festival, might be celebrated with a *wayang*, and in the past many *dalang* performed on such occasions in the same villages year after year, and their sons after them. Indeed, in the old days some *dalang* travelled a circuit of villages as the harvest came ripe. They performed village-sponsored plays to celebrate the harvest and were also available if any families, with their rice granaries full, wished to put on a performance in connection with a life-passage ritual.

A village-sponsored *wayang* is paid for by contributions collected from the head of every household in the village. Often the headman of a hamlet or village divides its households into three categories according to their wealth and, going from house to house, levies a contribution appropriate to each household's classification.

Although statistics are lacking, it appears that such communally sponsored *wayang* are diminishing in number. With the advent of new strains of rice, people living in the same community harvest their crop over a longer period, and more villagers can harvest two rather than only one crop of rice per year. The whole ritual dimension of rice growing seems to be fading, for that matter, and village-based rituals seem less common. Annual celebrations of Indonesian Independence Day, on 17 August, do take place in villages, and sometimes these are marked with *wayang*. But other performances that are easier to put on, such as athletic competitions and folk drama, are held more often than *wayang* in connection with Independence Day celebrations.

If communally sponsored performances are growing rarer, that has not threatened the livelihood of *dalang*, because with the increasing affluence of some portions of the Javanese populace it appears that more private families have the means to sponsor a performance now than in the past. In addition, it has become standard practice for government offices, universities, banks, and other institutions to sponsor performances to mark important events in that institution's history. On such occasions, high-level employees of the institution take the places of invited guests behind the screen, food is catered, and low-level employees may be pressed into service to help set up the space, serve the refreshments, etc.

No matter who the sponsors of a particular performance may be, it is important to note a fundamental fact about most *wayang*: their social embeddedness. Most people in the world today, including urban Indonesians, are used to paying cash for tickets to performances. Those tickets gain their buyers entry to a space usually set aside for such events, and the performances are usually conceived of as, among other things, money-making ventures. However personally we may think of our relations with our favourite performers, the sponsors (or 'producers') that arrange for their appearances are likely to be faceless partners to a transaction we take for granted. A great deal of money changes hands at a Javanese ritual celebration, and the relations among the sponsors of a performance, the *dalang*, and his troupe, are based on financial considerations. But *dalang* are quick to claim that making money is less important to them than providing instruction in the form of entertainment. And while invited guests have indeed made financial contributions to the event, they do not conceive of the invitation to see the play as a ticket they have bought either with money or foodstuffs given to the sponsors. Both contributions and invitations fit into a long history of exchanges between the two parties. Meanwhile, a greater number of people watch the performance from outside the sponsors' house, in which case there is no question of their having to pay.

Performances put on by institutions are something of an exception to the social embeddedness of *wayang*: they do not implicate the relations among families characteristic of privately sponsored performances. Nevertheless, they fit into another long-standing tradition, that of royal entertainments held to mark important occasions. The royal courts in Jogja and Solo still occasionally hold *wayang* that the public is free to attend.

Only in a few, atypical situations, such as when the national radio stations sponsor performances of shadow plays in enclosed halls, are Javanese accustomed to paying to attend. In most circumstances, a *wayang* is put on as a splendid display of the sponsors' largesse, something Westerners are at best familiar with when, for example, the Metropolitan Opera performs free concerts in New York's Central Park. And unlike in the Western tradition of support for the arts, at a *wayang* all of the invited guests and many of the casual spectators have personal connections to the sponsors and will recall long afterwards who it was that treated them to, say,

Ki Anom's brilliant rendering of 'Pandhu Crowned King'.

A family puts on a *wayang* as a bid for prestige. Villages do so as part of community-wide traditions thought to help assure prosperity and harmony. Government offices, banks, and other institutions sponsor performances as a means of furthering their image as pillars of society. In each case, a *wayang* brings honour upon its sponsors and pleasure to the community and thereby enters into the fabric of Javanese social life.

3
The Repertoire of Stories and the Structure of the Performance

MUCH about Ki Anom Soeroto's performance of 'Pandhu Crowned King' is representative of *wayang kulit* performances in general. Some of it is specific to that particular story, and to Ki Anom's particular telling of it. The story of Abyasa's selection of his successor fits into an enormous cycle of stories about his kin, and those stories make up the bulk of the *wayang* repertoire in Java today. At the same time, almost all performances follow a set structure of scenes much like the series of scenes that organized Ki Anom's telling of the story of Pandhu's coronation. Looking at the *wayang* repertoire more broadly, and pointing out the order of scenes that is common to virtually all performances, shows how much of the performance we have been considering is characteristic of other performances of *wayang* as well.

There are a very few *wayang* stories of purely Javanese origin. Those that are indigenous to Java deal with such mythic events as the original peopling of the island, the origins of rice, and the generation and eventual domestication of a frightening monster born out of the god Siva's semen. Few of these stories are performed very often in Java today, although the last-mentioned one, called *Murwakala*, is given in connection with a daytime performance-cum-ritual on behalf of people thought to be at risk of misfortune. Some stories native to Java that were performed annually as part of village-wide rituals are now falling into disuse as those rituals are abandoned.

In the past, many Javanese believed that the stories about Abyasa and his ancestors and descendants recounted the history of Java. Ancient temples on the Dieng Plateau (near Wonosobo in Central Java) are considered by some Javanese to this day to be the tombs of certain of Abyasa's grandsons and their servants. Most Javanese, however, have been taught that the stories are originally from India, and they are inclined to be non-committal on the subject of whether the events ever really happened anywhere.

In actual fact, the vast majority of shadow plays performed in Java relate stories based on one of the two great Indian epics, the *Ramayana* or the *Mahabharata*. It is impossible to know precisely how or when Java came to obtain this immense cache of stories. But it is clear that they have influenced Javanese arts for centuries, even as Javanese artists of all sorts have shaped the stories to their own purposes.

The *Mahabharata* is the more popular of the two epics in Java.[1] It contains hundreds of stories about several generations of characters whose lives intertwine in a complex history of heroism, deceit, and violence. Out of the welter of stories, Javanese focus their attention on those that concern the final two generations of heroes and their enemies, the Pandhawa and the Kurawa, whose civil war, the *Bratayuda*, brings the epic to a close. The story 'Pandhu Crowned King' narrates events before that period and is referred to by Javanese as an 'old story', meaning that it features the ancestors of the best-known characters, not those characters themselves. It is relatively rare for a *dalang* to give such a performance: many fear that the spectators will be disappointed if the figures they know best do not appear.

The antecedents of the *Bratayuda*, the concluding war, go far back before the story of Pandhu's coronation. But Abyasa's decision to give up his throne in favour of his second, not his eldest, son, provides the immediate impetus to that fratricidal conflict among his grandsons. Drestarata, Abyasa's blind son, sires 100 offspring, known collectively as the Kurawa. Pandhu has only five children, three sons by his first wife and two by his second. The five together are known as the Pandhawa, and they personify all the virtues of the warrior ethic. The eldest,

---

[1]This may not always have been the case. The temples at Prambanan in Central Java are decorated with stunning reliefs depicting scenes from the *Ramayana*.

Yudhistira, is supremely patient, honest, and judicious. The second, Bima, is larger and much less refined in appearance and manner (Colour Plate 16), but he always uses his great physical strength to champion righteousness. (Plate 19) The third son, Arjuna, is unrivalled in his attractiveness, his physical grace, and his martial skill, and in his capacity to bring spiritual force to bear in the effort to achieve any goal. The twins Nakula and Sadéwa, born to Pandhu's younger queen, have less sharply delineated character traits, but they are trusted and valiant assistants to their older half-brothers.

The Pandhawa's adherence to the code of conduct of warriors contrasts with the inclinations of their cousins, the Kurawa, who are given to greed, envy, and deceitfulness. The eldest of Drestarata's sons is Duryudana, whose own weaknesses are only exacerbated by the malevolent stratagems urged upon him by his counsellors, the potent but evil Priest Durna, and the equally devious prime minister of Ngastina, Arya Sangkuni. Fate offers these power-hungry characters an opportunity to test their nefarious skills, because Pandhu dies before his sons have grown and the Kurawa exercise authority over Ngastina as regents until the Pandhawa reach maturity. When that time arrives, however, Duryudana is persuaded by Priest Durna and Prime Minister Sangkuni to use every conceivable artifice to retain control over the kingdom. To make matters still worse, when the Pandhawa, banished to the forest, use their talents and virtue to build a kingdom of their own, Ngamarta, the Kurawa are filled with envy and wish to wrest it from them as well. The Kurawa's refusal to grant the Pandhawa the patrimony they are due, and the further insult of their demanding the kingdom that is the fruit of the Pandhawa's own labour, pits the Kurawa and Pandhawa against each other and leads to the carnage of the *Bratayuda*, a struggle in which both camps suffer tragically but that the gods themselves insist must occur.

Despite the outward simplicity of the central conflict between Abyasa's grandsons, an endless net of incidents, coincidences, and unexpected causal links ties the corpus of stories into an immense epic whole. But a great majority of shadow plays

19. Bima, one of the five Pandhawa brothers, tears his enemy, Dursasana, limb from limb. In a performance, there would be no background, but a puppeteer might fashion a special, cardboard puppet to rip apart in this climactic battle near the conclusion of the *Mahabharata*. (Drawing by Suharso)

narrate events during the time when the Pandhawa have established their kingdom in Ngamarta and stand poised to challenge the Kurawa for the return of Ngastina to their authority. That is why Javanese audiences are more likely to recognize the Kurawa, Pandhawa, and their respective children, kinsmen, and advisers, than characters from earlier parts of the cycle.

Although the moment just before the outbreak of the *Bratayuda* seems to intrigue Javanese most, few performances actually recount the events of that war. Some villages give annual performances of all or part of the *Bratayuda* in conjunction with a village purification or harvest ritual. This practice is usually justified on the grounds that the spirits of the villages' founders demand it. But it is considered very dangerous. The violence in the stories has always been thought powerful enough to unleash the forces of chaos in life, and few people have the nerve to ask a *dalang* to give such a performance.

Although the outlines of the epic stories, and even fine details about feuds and grudges that mark relations between particular characters, are clearly traceable to Indian sources, Javanese *dalang* have not been purely passive recipients of that heritage. They distinguish between 'principal stories' (*lakon pokok*) and 'branch stories' (*lakon carangan*). The former concern the great events of the epics, stories that must remain largely unchanged by their narrators, while the latter embellish that larger structure with imaginative additions. Puppeteers are enjoined to respect the basic character traits, kinship ties, and chronological sequence of events in the two epics, as well as the outline of the stories, but are free to make up branch stories of their own, weaving diverting and original patterns into the larger design.

Such stories may be played only a few times by a single *dalang*, or they may prove so popular and widely diffused as to become part of the permanent repertoire. However, these newer branch stories, including a great many for which Ki Anom Soeroto is famous, are actually less complex and less distinctive than many of the classical stories. 'Pandhu Crowned King' has a more elaborate plot than most branch stories, and because it recounts events that play a critical part in the later relations among Abyasa's descendants, it resonates much more deeply with the larger structure of the epic. Yet it is performed relatively rarely, crowded out by the lighter, simpler stories devised by contemporary *dalang*.

A common plot device in many newly invented stories, for example, turns on the attempt on the part of both the Pandhawa and the Kurawa to obtain a mystical boon, a *wahyu*, that will bring with it a guarantee of prosperity, well-being, and/or assurance of rule over a kingdom. Often a third party from across the sea is also in pursuit of the same *wahyu*. Such boons, however, cannot be won by force of arms or intrigue: they are granted only in recognition of superior spiritual potency, a self-denying control over all one's own desires and whims. The Pandhawa are models of such ascetic capacity while the Kurawa cannot do any more than go through the motions. People from across the sea are all known to be in the thrall of their own impulses—many a contemporary tourist confirms that long-held Javanese impression—and there is really no doubt about the outcome of such a story: the contender from the Pandhawa camp, usually Arjuna's son Angkawijaya, will win the *wahyu* in the end. But the *dalang* who creates any given version of this type of story can introduce various novel situations. Like a Hollywood Western, one then enjoys the variations on the same old themes and does not expect to be held in any suspense as to the ultimate result.

The few stories of indigenous, as opposed to Indic, origin, plus some versions of the *Bratayuda* stories, are the only ones that permit a puppeteer to structure a performance freely. All other performances follow a fixed pattern that gives them a surprising degree of consistency. Every performance begins with a long introduction in which the *dalang* describes a kingdom enjoying prosperity and peace, followed by a series of greetings among the people assembled at court. A matter of concern to the king and his courtiers is eventually broached, but no matter what the nature of that problem is, the king's return to his private chambers and the departure of the troops invariably follow the opening scene. A scene in another court comes next, followed by some skirmishes among troops sent out from the two kingdoms so far implicated in events. And so it goes: a scene in a hermitage, the humorous routines when the servants first appear, the knight's progress through the forest and encounter with an ogre in which the latter suffers the ultimate disgrace of dying by his own sword—all these scenes are included in every performance.

Performances given in the two Javanese court centres of Solo (or Surakarta) and Jogja (or Yogyakarta) differ in detail with regard to the fixed sequence of scenes. For example, in Jogjanese performances a battle develops out of the discussion in the first scene, whereas in Solo the first battle does not usually occur until later, after the scene introducing a second court. Other differences in stylistic detail distinguish language, dress, music, dance, and custom among the royal houses of Jogja and Solo and the people once subject to them. Those differences are still jealously maintained and they explain why, for example, Ki Anom Soeroto draws a large crowd when he performs in the region of Jogja but much larger ones when he performs in his native Solo, but they are not really fundamental.

Ki Anom Soeroto's telling of 'Pandhu Jumeneng Nata' (Pandhu Crowned King) is representative of much about other performances of *wayang kulit*. Another *dalang* would certainly perform it differently, and Ki Anom himself made many changes when he performed the same story for a different occasion. (For the radio he greatly reduced the comic elements and increased the moralizing ones, for example, Bagong's remarks about the need to stop meting out summary justice.) Nevertheless, the story fits into the larger story cycle of the *Mahabharata*, as do most stories performed in Javanese *wayang*, and the set order of scenes structured the performance just as it does virtually all performances, no matter what the story. Like most other *wayang*, too, this occasion was a noteworthy event in the sponsors' relations with other families. It remains to ask what deeper sense people might make of the performance, or really, of the *wayang* tradition overall. The next chapter will outline suggestions that have been made as to what *wayang* means.

4
What Might *Wayang* Mean?

An extravagantly beautiful and complicated art form, Javanese *wayang kulit* has long attracted the interest of people from outside Java. Many accounts have been provided, by foreign as well as Javanese commentators, to explain one or another facet of the genre.

Interpreting any art form opens on to controversy, and *wayang* is no exception to this rule. That so many ways of construing it have been proposed—some mutually contradictory, some complementary—demonstrates how rich, suggestive, and at the same time elusive, a performing art it is.

Javanese Commentaries

Javanese commentary on *wayang* tends to focus not on where the stories came from or what historical validity they might have, but rather on the moral lessons that might inhere in them all. In this reading, every story is reduced to a single progression in an individual's ethical development. A performance is taken to be analogous with the life-course. It starts from pregnancy and birth—equated with the music played before the play begins—and continues through the travails of youth—equated with the battles with ogres that take place during the middle section of every performance—and finally ends with the triumph of virtue both in a person's life and among the competing parties in a performance. What this interpretive approach really does is to disregard individual stories in favour of the fixed structure common to all performances, including the threefold division into sections (as distinguished by different musical modes) and the recurrence of certain invariant scenes.

Probably one reason many Javanese feel inclined to gloss stories in this way is because Java's religious history has removed the theological resonance the stories once had in Javanese culture. Ancient Java was deeply influenced by both Hindu and Buddhist teachings, as well as by indigenous ideas both about spirits that inhabit places and about spirits of one's ancestors that still hover about the living. Most Javanese lowlanders were eventually converted to Islam, however, and the Hindu gods ceased to be seen as the rulers of the cosmos. Stories about them could no longer be thought to account for the nature of the world. In place of the cosmological significance they had in the past, therefore, the Hindu myths had to be given some other sort of significance.

The result seems to represent a compromise between Javanese religious understandings, on the one hand, and their longstanding cultural inheritance, on the other. That is, Muslim doctrine replaced Hindu as an explanation of how the cosmos operates. But subjective experience could still be described in diverse kinds of imagery, and the Hindu myths as preserved and narrated in *wayang* eventually came to be seen, at least by some Javanese commentators, to refer to individual, psychological matters. *Wayang*, in this view, describes the moral progress of an individual as he or she comes to reach spiritual maturity.

This way of interpreting *wayang* does not, however, seem convincing to all Javanese. Strict Muslims in Java have long argued against Javanese practices intended to propitiate territorial and ancestral spirits, and some express disapproval of *wayang* as a heathen entertainment, one smacking of heterodox ideas and practices. When Ki Anom has Semar praise Pandhu's ascetic exercises in Seven Peaks, saying that doing so is not at all the same as praying to rocks and trees, he is defending Javanese practices from their religiously more orthodox detractors.

When non-Javanese ask, as many do, about the religious significance of *wayang*, it is difficult to come up with a simple response. Few Javanese are comfortable with a distinction Westerners make between secular and religious domains: ideas Westerners would classify as one or the other tend to be combined in Javanese thinking about experience. To the extent that Javanese do think in terms of formal religious doctrine, *wayang* does not enter into discussion: Muslim doctrine, or in the case of lesser numbers of people, Christian or other dogma, fulfils the definition of 'religion'. To the extent, though, that religion might imply a concern with either supernatural beings or with ethical matters, *wayang* could well be said to have religious overtones.

Many Javanese believe the landscape to be crowded with querulous and potentially troublesome spirits, and such spirits are thought particularly likely to interfere in humans' affairs at times of life-passage rituals. Providing spirits with offerings—a specially shaped mound of rice, some bananas, a coconut, etc.—helps dissuade them from attack. At a shadow play, such offerings are placed beneath the screen (Plate 20). However, Javanese ideas about spirits are somewhat vague, whereas the

20. Offerings are set out beneath the screen at a performance in order to placate any spirits that may inhabit particularly old puppets or musical instruments, or any other spirits—ancestral, territorial, or whatever—that may come upon the performance.

people that attend performances are immediately present. That makes the human audience rather more vivid to people's minds, especially the minds of performers and sponsors, than any spirits thought likely to be about. Furthermore, spirits are believed to cause upset and trouble, and people are apt to try to send them away rather than attract them. It would therefore be an exaggeration to say, as some Westerners have claimed, that spirits are the audience for which a performance is really intended.[1]

As for the ethical side of *wayang*, many Javanese, and certainly many *dalang*, believe the stories to contain moral teachings of great value, and of central importance to Javanese culture.[2] Concepts of moral responsibility, self-control, obligations to one's kin, and the consequences of one's actions, are all implicated in the stories *wayang* tell. To the extent that one wishes to label such lessons as 'religious', then a *wayang* performance has a religious dimension.

Rather than look for 'religious' meanings in shadow plays, however, it is really more fitting to see in them what Javanese often speak of as their most important quality: the way they illustrate both the importance of hierarchy in ordering social relations and every person's responsibility to respect that order by fulfilling his or her own role within it. Javanese society is profoundly shaped by understandings of people's 'place' (as in the English phrase, 'to know your place'), and any behaviour that flies in the face of such notions is very disturbing to many people. The world *wayang* presents to spectators is one even more consistently and irrevocably defined by hierarchy than everyday life. Most stories develop out of challenges or contraventions of the proper, that is to say, hierarchically ordered, way things are and are meant to be. The resolution of every plot is the neutralization of that threat to order in the world.

The whole conflict between the Pandhawa and the Kurawa develops because the elder line, the Kurawa, normally the hierarchically superior party, are born to a physically defective

---

[1] See, for example, the conclusion to Becker, 1979.
[2] See, for example, Sastroamidjojo, 1964, or Mulyono, 1977.

father and so lose their rights to Ngastina. It is easy to see why they would want to challenge the hierarchical ordering that results, yet they are wrong to do so.[3] In the course of the struggle between the Kurawa and the Pandhawa, meanwhile, a great cast of characters exemplifies in words and deeds the styles of interaction that go with status differences, differences that include all types of beings, whether human, divine, animal, or supernatural. To call this image of the world either religious or not would be to impose upon it categories foreign to Javanese thinking. It is an image of the world that is simply, and universally, hierarchical.

To respect hierarchy and fulfil one's responsibilities in the social order it sets up means, above all, to speak in a manner appropriate to one's own station and to the station of the person one addresses. Non-Javanese are often startled by the degree to which this issue of speaking in the proper style concerns Javanese. But Javanese see the ability to speak and to interact with the appropriate degree of formality as the defining characteristic of personal maturity. The Javanese language obliges a speaker to choose—every time he or she says anything at all—among a number of different words, all of which mean the same thing but imply different kinds of relations among speakers. *Wayang* illustrates this system of speech styles in all its precision and richness, thereby helping to maintain it, and many Javanese praise *wayang* and explain its unique prestige by reference to just that fact.[4]

Western Commentaries

Western analysts have looked for different sorts of information in *wayang*, and they have constructed a number of theories to account for its origins and for its significance in Javanese

---

[3] See Anderson, 1965, for a sensitive account of the moral ambiguities of the conflict, as well as the importance of hierarchy in all of *wayang*.

[4] A more complete discussion of Javanese interpretations of *wayang*, and of *wayang*'s place in Javanese society, is to be found in Keeler, 1987.

society. As in all matters intercultural, the debates within Western circles about *wayang* reflect the preoccupations and assumptions Westerners have brought to the subject.[5] A brief review of some of the major positions Westerners have taken points to shifts in Western intellectual history, as well as to contrasting ways of making sense of *wayang*.

Western scholarly interest in the genre goes back to the late eighteenth century, and it grew in the course of the nineteenth century, as more and more Westerners visited Java. Before he became Singapore's earliest developer, the colourful and resourceful Thomas Raffles was the lieutenant-governer of Java: his *History of Java*, published in 1817, attests to his interest in *wayang*. Dutch scholars soon started making available translations of texts of performances, although—disappointingly to modern scholars—they tended to omit the jokes and clowning routines that they thought insignificant. In line with the philological bent of nineteenth-century Orientalist scholarship, several Westerners devoted time and attention to searching for the sources in Indian literature of Javanese *wayang* stories, pointing out the deviations from Indian models to be found in Javanese versions of the epics.

Not just variants in the stories, but the relations between Javanese *wayang* and Indian and other prototypes more generally became the subject of debate among Western scholars by the end of the nineteenth century, and the debate continued well into the twentieth. Although the place of origin of the stories was never in doubt, it could not be decided where or why the basic technique of the performance arose. Could the Javanese simply have imitated an ancient Indian shadow puppet tradition, even if that tradition had disappeared in India? Could they, instead, have imitated the Chinese shadow play, since it is still performed in China, even though in general Chinese cultural influence in Java has been relatively slight?

---

[5]The Dutch *wayang* scholar, Victoria Clara van Groenendael, provides an excellent synopsis of these debates in the 'Introduction' to her annotated bibliography, 1987, pp. 11–21, and I am drawing on her work here.

The argument about the indigenous versus the Indian or Chinese origins of *wayang* precisely mirrors controversies about the prehistory of South-East Asia that continue to this day. It was long believed that such mainstays of South-East Asian societies as rice and metal-working were introduced to the region from the supposedly culturally and technologically more dynamic neighbouring civilizations of India and China. This representation of South-East Asia as the passive recipient of outside influences, rather than as the active creator of its own heritage, permeated the colonial powers' vision of the region. Whether consciously or unconsciously, it helped justify the colonialists' presence as the virile force needed to make the area bear fruit.[6] In recent years, archaeological work, particularly in mainland South-East Asia, has contested the view that rice or metal-working need necessarily have developed elsewhere,[7] and in any case the possibility of independent invention in several regions is not to be ruled out. The whole argument about where certain technological methods were first adopted suggests an anachronistic application of nationalistic or communal concerns—competition for glory among rival ethnic groups or national populations—to questions that are based on faulty assumptions. The domestication of rice, for example, was not a sudden invention to be claimed by one person or group of persons. It was not a contest in which we can, with hindsight, declare certain people the winners.

It is not surprising, however, that when they turned to consider the prehistory of *wayang*, Western scholars were apt to assume by the same sorts of reasoning that South-East Asia depended on foreign traditions for cultural stimuli. The emphasis on texts in Western approaches to Asian civilization, following the pioneering work on Sanskrit in the eighteenth century, meant that places with the largest quantities of writing as well as the longest tradition of writing practices—and in Asia this meant India and China—appeared to be the founts of all

---

[6]See on this point Peterson, 1982–3.
[7]See Higham, 1989.

civilization. Furthermore, Java could be seen to have borrowed heavily from India with respect to religious ideas. It was easy to conclude that Java had borrowed much of everything else.

Claims for the Indian origin of the practice of projecting images upon a screen appeared stronger when it was found that shadow plays were performed in southern India. Already in the nineteenth century, however, some scholars thought that the genre must have been created by the Javanese themselves. This claim was supported by reference to the vocabulary describing the basic tools of the *dalang*'s craft, such as the name of the coconut-oil lamp that was the traditional light source: the word, *bléncong*, is not of Indic origin. Neither, for that matter, is the word *dalang*.

The debate about the origins of *wayang* was linked to speculation about its original purpose or function. An eminent Dutch scholar, Hazeu, suggested at the end of the last century that the whole genre developed out of a cult in honour of the spirits of the ancestors.[8] Rituals surrounding death are numerous in Java, as indeed they are throughout Indonesia. Every Javanese who dies beyond infancy is honoured by ceremonies observed on the day of death, three days later, seven days later, forty days later, 100 days later, one year later, two years later, and 1,000 days after the date of death. This profusion of funerary observances—by no means the most elaborate or extensive in the region—is indicative of how important many South-East Asian peoples, including Javanese, believe relations between the living and the dead to be. It seemed evident to many Dutch scholars that *wayang* must fit in with this preoccupation with one's ancestors. Indeed, it was felt that the shadow figures themselves probably originally represented the spirits of the ancestors, and only later came to be identified with the characters of the Indic epics, as Hindu influence suffused Javanese culture.

The problem with such reconstructions of the original or essential nature of *wayang* is that they are virtually impossible

[8] See Hazeu, 1897.

to verify. Javanese today certainly do not look upon the shadows cast upon the screen as the spirits of their ancestors. Actually, some Javanese think that the first propagators of Islam in Java—the so-called *Wali Sanga*—originated, or at least developed, *wayang* as a means of spreading Muslim teachings and converting people to the religion. This view seems hardly credible, both on the grounds of historical chronology and on the grounds that the message of Islam stands counter to the Hindu-based image of the cosmos inherent to the world of *wayang*. Yet, because so little evidence exists concerning *wayang* in Java in the past, no theory can be either accepted or rejected out of hand. Once again, the preconceptions and preoccupations of the analysts necessarily inform every suggestion as to *wayang*'s essence. To cite two somewhat outrageous examples, one Dutch scholar saw in a *wayang* performance vestiges of initiation rites carried out in an originally totemistic Javanese society,[9] while another[10] saw phallic implications in such details as the large thumbs of certain figures, including Bima, related to the god of the winds! Initiation rites, totemism, and phallic symbols were all in the air in Western intellectual circles at the turn of the century, and it is not surprising that they cropped up in theories about the meaning of *wayang*.

Another favoured suggestion about *wayang* among Western commentators would have it that they afford *dalang* an opportunity to engage in political criticism—this in a society that has otherwise always severely restricted political expression. By veiled allusions in the story-line and sly comments put in the mouths of 'foolish' servants, it is claimed, *dalang* can make political points without fear of reprisal. The image of *dalang* making subversive comments and getting away with it is appealing to anyone who favours freedom of expression over uncritical acceptance of authority. At a very local level, *dalang* probably do make covert references to familiar political figures, and at times of dynastic change or upheaval in Javanese history

[9]Rassers, 1922.
[10]Serrurier, 1896.

wayang probably did become a means of more daring political expression. In the 1950s and early 1960s, when Indonesian society became divided into intensely competing political factions, *wayang* certainly was drawn into the general politicization of Javanese life. Nevertheless, it would be an exaggeration to think that most *dalang* engage in the risks of political controversy today, that they did so routinely in the past, or that spectators expect to find examples of such resistance to established authority in many performances they attend. To treat *wayang* as a form of political expression would also be unduly reductionist, since it would explain a complex art form with reference to only one kind of meaning.

More central to the *wayang* tradition than any essential 'meaning' is the aesthetic pleasure it affords its spectators by means of the compelling quality of its images, the beauty of its music, the complexity of its stories, and the enveloping atmosphere of a night-long, deliberately paced entertainment. Some of these very qualities, particularly the last one, seem out of kilter with the society Java is now becoming, and raise questions about whether *wayang* can remain a viable art form—questions that will be addressed in the concluding chapter.

5
An Ancient Art Form in the Modern World

ARE shadow plays an archaic art form, destined to be lost in a modern national culture? Or are they as resilient now as they must have been in the past to survive over so many centuries? Indonesia is undergoing rapid economic and social change, and Java lies at the heart of those changes. It is an open question how developments that are modifying everything about life in both rural and urban Java will affect the *wayang* tradition. But it is worth considering some of those changes as we ask what place *wayang* might have in Javanese society in the future.

The most striking changes that have taken in place in Java over the past twenty years or so can be symbolized by three things: a village schoolhouse, a light bulb, and a motor bike. The schools that have been built in enormous numbers throughout Java over that time are part of an explosion in educational opportunities for young Javanese. The rural electrification programme has brought light bulbs into many village homes: it is one of many changes taking place in the circumstances of village life in this traditionally agrarian society. And motor bikes make up one of the most desired items in the vastly expanded consumer market. Of course, many other changes, such as agricultural development and urbanization, are critical parts of Java's recent and ongoing history. But they do not bear on the future of *wayang* quite as directly as do education, electrification, and consumerism.

Education in Java means education in the national language of Indonesian. Indonesian is closely related to Javanese, but the two languages are not mutually intelligible. Literacy rates have risen dramatically in Java in the recent past, and there is an enormous pool of young Javanese with elementary, secondary, and even college education. These young people know

Indonesian far better than their parents. But few of them know the 'literary' vocabulary of Javanese—not just the vocabulary of literature but also that of flowery, deliberately archaized speech—as well as their older kin do. *Wayang* draws on this vocabulary in the *dalang*'s narrative descriptions, and in some of the formal greetings among characters. To lose the ability to understand it does not really undercut spectators' enjoyment of the performance, since the characters themselves speak a readily intelligible Javanese. But the impression that *wayang* contains a great deal of obscure language can make some younger Javanese, especially urban ones, shy away from it. Books and performances in Indonesian, in contrast, appeal to young people because they seem appropriate to their status as educated, modern citizens.

Light bulbs are often welcomed by rural Javanese parents with the remark that now their children will be able to study their lessons more easily and cheaply than they could when they relied on kerosene lamps. But just as importantly, electricity in village homes means that people can plug in television sets. Only a small percentage of Javanese have the money to buy a television, of course, but neighbours gather at the homes of people who do have them to watch the news and whatever programmes are on. Indeed, electricity, education, and command of the Indonesian language open up a world of entertainment previously little known to most Javanese, such as television, movies, and pop music. Indonesia has a flourishing film industry, and many Western, Chinese, and Indian films are also shown in Indonesian theatres. The television industry is growing, and Indonesian pop music is well-established.

Mention of these genres that developed originally in the West should not suggest that Javanese cultural and artistic traditions are simply eclipsed by them. Among rural Javanese—and probably a good many urban ones—the most popular television programme is the once-weekly folk drama (*kethoprak*) show, broadcast in Javanese and in a manner very true to that genre's conventions. Indonesian movies may look a lot like their Hollywood cousins, right down to the flashy cars and luxurious sets, but the turns of the plot, responding as they do to Indonesian expectations, can surprise the non-Indonesian with a different sense of what makes moral and aesthetic sense.[1] Indonesian pop music, too, may sound like a musically simplified version of a lot of Western songs, and some South Asian ones, but the lyrics often address time-honoured Javanese concerns about keeping a steady grip on things even in the face of hardship or heartache.

To enjoy any of these art forms does not preclude enjoying *wayang*. Many people enjoy several different genres. But between *wayang* and electronic media there is a major aesthetic difference: in their timing. A *wayang* moves at quite a slow pace. The interludes of stately *gamelan* music, the long discussions among figures at court, the *dalang*'s lines of sung verse, all follow a rhythm very different from the scenes—timed in seconds—that are characteristic of the electronic media. Folk drama produced on television straddles the divide between traditional and electronic media and illustrates the difference vividly: on television, its scenes move very quickly, whereas most live performances proceed just as deliberately, indeed meander just as casually, as a *wayang* can. It seems possible that Javanese who grow up around television and movies will come to lose the taste for *wayang*, with its slow, deliberate, internal mechanic.

Even if the audience for shadow plays remains large and loyal, there is another question: how many families will continue to sponsor performances when there are so many consumer goods on which to spend their money? In the past, a big, impressive ritual celebration was a dramatic demonstration of a family's wealth and social standing. That is still true, and the truly wealthy can put on such a display without sacrificing the satisfaction of other needs or wishes. For many Javanese families, however, choices have to be made. If putting on a *wayang* reflects well on their standing, riding a bicycle does not: investing money in a motor bike may well take precedence

---

[1] See on this point Heider, 1991.

over the less palpable return investing in a *wayang* might bring one's image in the community. There are also such investments as children's education to consider. A college education, or even a high school education for children who have failed to gain admission to the cheaper but more competitive state-run schools, can strain many a family's finances, leaving no excess funds for big ritual celebrations.

It seems likely that very wealthy Javanese will continue to sponsor *wayang* to mark such occasions as their daughters' weddings. What seems less likely is that Javanese of comfortable but not really substantial wealth will be as ready on similar occasions to expend the great sums of money that hiring a famous *dalang* and his troupe requires. Less famous puppeteers, of course, could be hired for much less money. That still happens: there are many respected and popular *dalang*, outside the ranks of the top five or six Jogjanese and Solonese ones everyone has heard of, who still perform often in Java and do so for relatively modest fees. But mounting a *wayang* means not just paying the *dalang* and his troupe, but also providing food for all the guests, and all the many people whose assistance will be needed to set up the performing area, etc. It is always a fairly costly undertaking.

The electronic media, furthermore, have already affected people's standards. Cassettes of the best performances by the late Ki Nartosabdho, Ki Anom Soeroto, and Ki Jaka Raharja, who are some of the most famous of Solo's stars, and of the great story-teller Ki Timbul, and of the hilariously inventive Ki Hadisugito, who are among Jogja's favourites, are played constantly over loudspeakers in Java. People who could never afford to put on a real performance when they marry off a daughter, say, or circumcise a son, rent a tape recorder, tapes, and loudspeakers and broadcast the sound of a *wayang* throughout the night. This has raised everyone's aesthetic expectations. People proclaim themselves unwilling to go to a performance by a less-accomplished *dalang* now, accustomed as they are to hearing the powerful voices and hilarious routines of the top stars. Why, to draw an analogy in Western art forms, would one go down the street to hear local talent sing *Traviata* when one can listen to Maria Callas's definitive version on compact disc? Yet the long-term consequences of such rising expectations could be dire. If younger *dalang* lack opportunities to develop their skills in countless performances near their homes the way their ancestors had, fewer really accomplished *dalang* are likely to be around in the future—much as it is claimed that the dearth of great Italian opera singers at present can be blamed on the loss of the local singing traditions in modern Italy.

If demand for less illustrious *dalang* falters, then eventually supply will as well. Most *dalang* have been born to the tradition: they have been the sons of *dalang*, and have watched—and fallen asleep—behind their fathers at countless performances from infancy. As they grow older, aspiring *dalang* play in the orchestra, having learned all the music by hearing it countless times. Then they may start performing on their own, either for daytime performances or when their fathers must refuse a request to perform on a particular night because of a prior engagement. Not all sons of *dalang* choose to pursue their fathers' path, of course, not all that do come to equal their fathers' skills and popularity, and not all successful *dalang* have been born to *dalang*. But this pattern has characterized the transmission of the art form for centuries.

Today, when young men consider whether pursuing a career as a performer appeals to them, they must weigh, as must their parents, whether they might not do better getting a job in the civil service, long thought to be the most secure and most prestigious of careers. A few of them might find their artistic skills useful, such as in a government office whose staff would like to have a *gamelan* instructor in their midst. Most would, instead, leave the Javanese arts behind them as they put on the khaki uniform of the bureaucrat. Personal inclinations still enter into their calculations, of course. One *dalang* in a village in the Klaten area, by way of example, had six sons. Of them, the eldest became a *dalang* in his own right but died young, one became a civil servant in the provincial capital, one was an accomplished musician but not much interested in becoming a *dalang*, one went off to Kalimantan to teach school, one hoped to earn a college degree in forestry, which would presumably lead to a career in the civil service, and one was determined to become a *dalang* come what may.

In this century, schools have been established to train *dalang*. Diplomas from court-sponsored or, more recently, state-run academies win much prestige for their possessors, and some *dalang* send their sons off to such institutions for just that reason. None the less, few people truly believe that a *dalang*'s skills can be learned in a classroom. Schools may claim the authority to establish the proper way to perform, but most families of *dalang* are unconvinced that their own traditions are faulty. The fate of art school graduates will not really determine the fate of the *dalang*'s art.

Where the schools might eventually prove more influential lies in the reforms some teachers have introduced in performance practice. The state-run performing arts school in Solo (Sekolah Tinggi Seni Indonesia or STSI) has put on *wayang* reduced to only a few hours playing time, some of the plays in Indonesian rather than in Javanese. So far these mini-versions of *wayang*, stripped of many of the set pieces that fill the hours of a night-long performance, have failed to win a wide audience. Conceivably, however, they could prove attractive to urban sponsors worried about getting to the office the next morning.

Javanese *wayang* seems in no way endangered. It is still far too popular among millions of Javanese to disappear. Performances may become somewhat rarer, maybe even briefer, although few true *aficionados* would be satisfied were a performance not to end in the mysterious half-light of dawn. Still, *wayang* has fascinated Javanese and non-Javanese for so long that it is hard to imagine spending many nights in the dry season in Java without hearing a man's voice singing long phrases against the background of the *gamelan*'s soft, velvety sound.

Select Bibliography

Anderson, B., *Mythology and the Tolerance of the Javanese*, Ithaca, NY, Cornell Modern Indonesia Project, 1965.

Becker, A. L., 'Text-Building, Epistemology, and Aesthetics in Javanese Shadow Theatre', in A. L. Becker and A. A. Yengoyan (eds.), *The Imagination of Reality: Essays in Southeast Asian Coherence Systems*, Norwood, NJ, Ablex, 1979, pp. 211–43.

Clara van Groenendael, V., *Wayang Theatre in Indonesia: An Annotated Bibliography*, Dordrecht, Foris Publications, 1987.

Hazeu, G., *Bijdragen tot de kennis van het Javaansche tooneel*, Leiden, Brill, 1897.

Heider, K., *Indonesian Cinema: National Culture on Screen*, Honolulu, University of Hawaii Press, 1991.

Higham, C., *The Archaeology of Mainland Southeast Asia*, Cambridge, Cambridge University Press, 1989.

Keeler, W., *Javanese Shadow Plays, Javanese Selves*, Princeton, Princeton University Press, 1987.

Mulyono, S., *Human Characters in the Wayang*, trans. M. Medeiros, Jakarta, Pustaka Wayang, 1977.

Peterson, W., 'Colonialism, Culture History, and Southeast Asian Prehistory', *Asian Perspectives*, 25(1), 1982–3, pp. 123–32.

Rassers, W., *De Panji Roman*, Antwerpen, De Vos-van Kleef, 1922.

Sastroamidjojo, A. Seno, *Renungan tentang pertundjukan wajang kulit*, Jakarta, Kinta, 1964.

Serrurier, L., *De wajang poerwa: eene ethnologische studie*, Leiden, Brill, 1896.

Zoetmulder, P., *Kalangwan: A Survey of Old Javanese Literature*, The Hague, Martinus Nijhoff, 1974.